I0096466

Workkeys Workplace Documents Test Prep Study Guide with Practice Tests for NCRC Certification

The Workkeys examination is a trademark of ACT Inc, which is not affiliated with nor endorses this publication.

Workkeys Workplace Documents Test Prep Study Guide with Practice Tests for NCRC Certification

© COPYRIGHT 2022. Exam SAM Study Aids & Media dba www.examsam.com

All rights reserved. No part of this publication may be reproduced, stored in a retrieval system, or transmitted, in any form or by any means, electronic, mechanical, photocopying, recording, or otherwise, without the prior written permission of the copyright owner.

ISBN-13: 978-1-949282-82-5

The Workkeys examination is a trademark of ACT Inc, which is not affiliated with nor endorses this publication.

Table of Contents

WORKKEYS WORKPLACE DOCUMENTS PRACTICE TEST 1

Instructions: Read each of the passages below and then answer the questions that follow each one. Select only ONE answer per question. There is no penalty for incorrect answers, so you should guess an answer choice even when you are unsure. You are allowed 55 minutes to answer all 35 questions.

Bernards' Department Stores (Level 3)

Employee Notice

Employees must be well-groomed and well-dressed. Clothing must be in good order, without rips, tears, holes, or stains.

Clothing must be professional and appropriate for work. Lounge wear, leisure wear, and work out clothing must not be worn. Clothing styles based on an employee's religion or race are permitted.

Your employee badge must be worn at all times while you are on shift. You cannot work without one, and you will not get paid for that day. If you need to order a new badge, please inform Susan in HR. New badges cost each employee $25.

Question 1: You work for Bernards' Department Store. The main purpose of this document is to:
- A. set forth the mission statement of the company.
- B. instruct employees on how to dress for work.
- C. state that clothing based on religious beliefs is permitted.
- D. warn employees that clothing must not be torn.
- E. inform employees of their contact person in HR.

Question 2: According to the document, which of the following is not necessary if you lose your badge?
- A. paying for a replacement.
- B. telling Susan before your shift starts.
- C. taking the day off without pay.
- D. contacting the designated person in HR.
- E. filing a form to report the loss.

© COPYRIGHT 2022. Exam SAM Study Aids & Media dba www.examsam.com
This material may not be copied or reproduced in any form.

Spa Admission Policy (4)

Any club member who has an Elite Status Card will now get discounts off the price of guest admissions. Please follow the guidelines given below:

Guest admissions for meals

- The member must accompany his or her guest for the meal.

- If the member does not show their Elite Status Card, please ask them to do so.

- Note down the price of the guest's food and drink on the "guest discount for meals" ticket.

- Write your signature and the date on the 10% Guest Discount for Meals Ticket and place it in the accounting department in-box.

- The meal discount can only be offered between 11 am and 11 pm.

Guest admissions for the spa

- The member must accompany his or her guest for the spa treatment.

- If the member does not show their Elite Status Card, please ask them to do so.

- Use the cash register to take 20% off the price of the guest's spa treatment.

- Initial the receipt.

- The spa discount can be offered any time the spa is open.

© COPYRIGHT 2022. Exam SAM Study Aids & Media dba www.examsam.com
This material may not be copied or reproduced in any form.

Question 3: You work in the restaurant. What should you write on the appropriate ticket?

    A. 10% off

    B. Guest discount for meals

    C. Your signature and the date

    D. Accounting department

    E. 20% Off

Question 4: You work in the spa. A non-member guest has come to the spa alone and is requesting admission. What should you do?

    A. ask for their Elite Status Card.

    B. tell them about the discount.

    C. initial their receipt.

    D. inform them that they must come with a member.

    E. note down the appropriate information on their ticket.

© COPYRIGHT 2022. Exam SAM Study Aids & Media dba www.examsam.com
This material may not be copied or reproduced in any form.

INSTRUCTIONS FOR THE SHIPPING DEPARTMENT (Level 4)

Special Instructions for International Orders

Four large rectangular containers have been placed by the rear door of the shipping room. In the middle of the room, we have placed a special staging station for CHA-4 international orders. All of the packages to be shipped internationally, whether large or small, will be placed in the staging area by the packaging department. Each of these packages must be placed into the appropriate container as follows:

- Container A is for packages that weigh 16 ounces or less.

- Container B for packages with a weight of over 16 ounces, up to 32 ounces.

- Container C is for packages that weigh more than 32 ounces but less than 80 ounces.

- Container D is for all packages that are 80 ounces or more in weight.

- Container E is for packages that have been damaged. These will be sent back to the packaging department, causing the order to be delayed by 2 days.

If the packages are not sorted correctly, they will not be able to be weighed and will be rejected for shipping. In this case, the shipment of the customer's order will be delayed more than five days. This will very negatively affect our online customer ratings, and we cannot afford for this to happen.

© COPYRIGHT 2022. Exam SAM Study Aids & Media dba www.examsam.com
This material may not be copied or reproduced in any form.

Question 5: In the first paragraph of the instructions, the term CHA-4 most likely refers to:

    A. a category of international orders.

    B. part of the rear door.

    C. an area of the shipping room.

    D. a type of large rectangular container.

    E. packages that weigh more than 80 ounces.

Question 6: According to the instructions, what could cause a customer's order to be delayed more than two days?

    A. A package is not sorted correctly by its shape

    B. An 80-ounce package is placed in Container D

    C. A 16-ounce damaged package is placed in Container E.

    D. A 32-ounce damaged package is placed in Container B.

    E. A 16-ounce package is placed in container A.

© COPYRIGHT 2022. Exam SAM Study Aids & Media dba www.examsam.com
This material may not be copied or reproduced in any form.

Reporting on-site accidents (Level 5)

The incident report form must be used to report accidents, injuries, and medical situations. (Incidents involving employee aggression or assault should be reported directly to the Human Resources Manager.) In all cases, the report should be completed within 24 hours of the event. Your completed forms should be submitted to the Vice President of Human Resources.

The report must include the full name and date of birth of the person harmed in the incident. The date, time, location, and description of incident (what happened, how it happened, and any other factors leading to the event) must also be included. Be as specific as possible and attach additional sheets if needed for the description.

On Part A, describe the injury sustained (bruise, laceration, sprain, broken bone), the part of body injured, and any other information known about the resulting injury. Also describe what type of first aid was administered on site and whether the injured person was taken to the hospital. If the person was admitted to the hospital, the name of the hospital should also be provided on Part B of the form.

© COPYRIGHT 2022. Exam SAM Study Aids & Media dba www.examsam.com
This material may not be copied or reproduced in any form.

Question 7: According to the document, who always receives information about onsite accidents?
- A. the Vice President of Human Resources
- B. the Human Resources Manager
- C. the local hospital
- D. the employee's manager
- E. the head of the employee's department

Question 8: For which one of the following reasons would extra pages need to be attached to the incident report?
- A. to indicate the name of the hospital
- B. to provide further details about how the incident occurred
- C. to describe the injury the employee suffered
- D. to indicate the date, time, and location of the incident
- E. to provide the employee's name and birth date

© COPYRIGHT 2022. Exam SAM Study Aids & Media dba www.examsam.com
This material may not be copied or reproduced in any form.

Memo To: All Members of The Hospitality Team (Level 5)

From: Juna Smith, General Manager

Please follow the procedures in this memo for all guests reserving rooms at our hotel:

Deposits
Guests are required to pay a $10 deposit per room per night in order to make a reservation.

Our agreement to accommodate a guest is a legal contract and any deposit paid by the guest to reserve a room is not refundable under any circumstances.

Cancellation
We adhere to a strict 48-hour cancellation policy. If a reservation is canceled 48 hours or more prior to a proposed stay, we agree not to charge for the room in full.

If a guest cancels less than 48 hours in advance of the proposed stay and the room is later filled by a walk-in booking, the guest will not be charged the balance of the price of the room.

In the event that the guest cancels less than 48 hours in advance, has prepaid the price of the room, and the room is later filled by a walk-in booking, we will refund the price of the room minus the deposit to them.

If a guest cancels less than 48 hours in advance of the proposed stay and we do not succeed in re-booking the room, the guest will not be liable for the full balance, but there will be a 30% cancellation fee and a 10% administration fee.

Pets
Well-behaved pets are permitted by prior arrangement only and at the additional cost of $10 per pet per night.

Other charges
The price of the accommodation includes the room, linens, swimming pool access, and breakfast. The guest is to be charged for ice and for items from the mini-bar.

© COPYRIGHT 2022. Exam SAM Study Aids & Media dba www.examsam.com
This material may not be copied or reproduced in any form.

Question 9: What cost is incurred by a guest who cancels their reservation 72 hours in advance?

    A. they will have to pay a cancellation fee.

    B. the cost of the deposit will be deducted from their fees.

    C. they will not be charged if another guest takes the room.

    D. no cost is incurred by the guest.

    E. they will lose their $10 deposit.

Question 10: Based on the memo shown, a cancellation will cost a guest the greatest amount of money when:

    A. it is made more than 48 hours in advance of the stay.

    B. it is made less than 48 hours in advance of the stay and the room is not filled by a walk-in.

    C. he or she has prepaid the full price of the room.

    D. he or she had planned on bringing a pet.

    E. a deposit has been paid.

© COPYRIGHT 2022. Exam SAM Study Aids & Media dba www.examsam.com
This material may not be copied or reproduced in any form.

Shipping Instruction Checklist (Level 6)

Please be advised that the following information must be included on each shipment:

Shipper Name (SN) – This is the name of the customer requesting the shipment.

Pickup Party (PU) – This is the name of the party responsible for collecting the order after the shipment by road or rail. If it is a rail shipment, provide the name of the rail facility or station that will send the shipment. The PU is only required for pick-ups by road if the PU differs from the SN.

Origin (ON) – All rail shipments must be identified as domestic origin (DO) or international origin (IO). For truck, van, or carload shipments, origin identification may be omitted.

Consignee Name (CN) or Care of Party (C1) – CN is the name of the original owner of the goods or the equipment. C1 indicates that the goods will be shipped to a different party. The name of either party as well as CN or C1 should be listed on the shipping form. In addition, the original owner shall bear responsibility for the goods until they reach their destinations. Therefore, CN or C1 parties should be advised to insure the goods or equipment accordingly.

Destination (DN) – Provide the city and state for rail shipments and the street address, city, and ZIP code for road shipments.

Standard Transportation Commodity Code (STCC) – This 7-digit number must be written on the shipping form.

Route (RT) – These are our carrier and junction abbreviations, including origin and destination delivery switch carriers, when applicable.

Payment Method (PM) – Indicate whether the shipment is prepaid (PP) or payment upon receipt (PUR).

Weight Code (WC) – This is according to our shipment scale weight. RL scale weight means that the load is of regular weight. OL scale weight means that the load is too heavy and additional fees must be paid before shipment may be undertaken.

© COPYRIGHT 2022. Exam SAM Study Aids & Media dba www.examsam.com
This material may not be copied or reproduced in any form.

Hazmat (HM) Information – Use only if a hazardous commodity is being shipped. The HM number, primary hazardous class, and proper chemical name must also be provided.

Question 11: Which of the following acronyms refers to a person who receives goods who is not the original owner of the goods?
- A. SN
- B. DN
- C. C1
- D. CN
- E. HM

Question 12: Which one of the following two codes may not be required in certain situations?
- A. PU and HM
- B. SN and HM
- C. PU and DN
- D. CN and WC
- E. C1 and RT

© COPYRIGHT 2022. Exam SAM Study Aids & Media dba www.examsam.com
This material may not be copied or reproduced in any form.

Conveyor Belt Instructions (Level 6)

<u>Adjustments:</u> Conveyor belt tracking is set prior to the goods leaving our factory. Should the tracking of the belt need to be set or adjusted, please undertake the following steps in the order provided: Loosen the side plate screws, bring up the tension of the belt with the adjusting screw, and tighten the side plate screws. Note that operators should not attempt to adjust the speed of the belt further as attempting to do so may cause damage to the lagged pulley system.

<u>During operation:</u> The removal of safety equipment, such as covers and safety guards, during operation is prohibited. Likewise, the hazard areas at the beginning and end of the belt must be secured by lowering the respective protective flaps. Approaching and/or operating the machine is only allowed for persons wearing suitable clothing, which includes hair net, ear protection, and safety shoes.

<u>Placing Out of Operation:</u> When placing the belt out of operation, be especially careful to avoid injury by electric shock. Before the machine is put out of operation, make sure it has completely stopped moving and is unplugged before any remedial works are carried out. When placing out of operation, the machine must be left in a safe state according to the procedures specified by the CHSG.

<u>Storage of the Belt:</u> Preparation for storage and actual physical storage of the conveyor is only to be carried out by a fully qualified person who has completed the Company's Conveyor Belt Training Course.

<u>Safety Compliance:</u> In the event that any usual activity should appear with any of the mechanisms or in any of the procedures mentioned above, the employee should inform a member of the senior management team immediately before taking any other action.

© COPYRIGHT 2022. Exam SAM Study Aids & Media dba www.examsam.com
This material may not be copied or reproduced in any form.

Question 13: You are the machine operator. You have noticed that the conveyor belt has suddenly started to run at an unusually fast speed. What action should you undertake first?

    A. Unplug the machine as quickly as you can.

    B. Wait for the belt to stop moving.

    C. Report it to a superior right away.

    D. Try to avoid damaging the lagged pulley system.

    E. Change the tension of the belt by loosening the adjusting screw.

Question 14: Which one of the following is most likely the Company's primary rationale behind the issuance of this document?

    A. to reduce the number of work-related accidents and injuries caused by the conveyor belt.

    B. to inform employees about the order of the steps necessary in order to adjust the conveyor belt.

    C. to prevent electric shocks from the conveyor belt, which has been on the rise recently.

    D. to tell employees about the Company's Conveyor belt training course.

    E. to clarify the procedures applicable to operating and storing the conveyor belt.

© COPYRIGHT 2022. Exam SAM Study Aids & Media dba www.examsam.com
This material may not be copied or reproduced in any form.

Tax Filing Instructions (Level 6)

Effective this tax year, taxpayers will no longer need to choose between the Short Tax Form (STF) or Long Tax Form (LTF). Instead, all individual taxpayers are now required to prepare and file the newly-designed Universal Tax Form (UTF), which has ten new numbered schedules, in addition to the existing alphabetical schedules, such as Schedules X, Y, and Z. If a taxpayer's return is complicated, as is the case, for example, when certain deductions or credits are being claimed or additional taxes are owing, then the taxpayer will need to complete one or more of the new numbered schedules. However, many taxpayers will only need to complete and file the UTF without attaching any of the schedules.

The following list provides general guidance regarding which schedule or schedules many taxpayers will need to file based on their individual circumstances. For further information, taxpayers or return preparers should peruse the UTF General Instructions and Guidance Booklet for more information.

Note that the following list is for individual tax returns only. Corporate or partnership filers are required to file a Business Tax Form (BTF) rather than a UTF.

SCHEDULE 1 – This schedule is to be used when the taxpayer has income in addition to wages and salaries from employment, such as gains from the sale of a property, rental income, or interest income. Note that, contrary to a common misbelief, unemployment compensation, prizes, and gambling winnings are taxable and should be reported on this schedule.

SCHEDULE 2 – This schedule is for taxpayers that are self-employed, earning an income from the operation of a non-incorporated or non-partnership business. Self-employed taxpayers should report business income and itemized business expenses and deductions on this schedule.

SCHEDULE 3 – This schedule is required if the taxpayer owes a tax in addition to income tax, such as Capital Gains Tax payable upon the sale of a property. It

© COPYRIGHT 2022. Exam SAM Study Aids & Media dba www.examsam.com
This material may not be copied or reproduced in any form.

is also required if the filer is a foreign entity or third-party designee or paid preparer.

SCHEDULE 4 – The taxpayer should use this schedule if eligible to claim tax credits. Refundable tax credits will be paid by check or into the taxpayer's bank account. Please see the RTCB for further information on claiming tax credits.

Question 15: Which one of the following inferences is most likely true, according to the document?
- A. The change in the tax forms is an attempt to simplify the system.
- B. Most taxpayers will not need to file any schedules.
- C. Instructions for certain new schedules have not been provided in this document.
- D. It is a common problem that partnerships mistakenly file a UTF instead of a BTF.
- E. Most people try to hide their gambling winnings.

Question 16: Based on the information in the last paragraph of these instructions, the RCTB is most likely:
- A. a set of laws that accountants have to follow.
- B. an authoritative taxation body.
- C. an attachment to Schedule 4.
- D. a separate instructional booklet.
- E. an amendment to the UTF.

Question 17: You are an accountant and work as a paid preparer of individual tax returns. A client informs you that in addition to their salary, they have sold a property and want to claim a tax credit called the "self-employment tax" credit. What forms and schedules should you file for this client?
- A. Form UTF and Schedules 1, 2, 3 & 4
- B. Form UTF and Schedules 1, 3 & 4
- C. Form UTF and Schedules 1, 2 & 4
- D. Form UTF and Schedules 1, 2 & 3
- E. Form UTF and Schedules 1 & 4

© COPYRIGHT 2022. Exam SAM Study Aids & Media dba www.examsam.com
This material may not be copied or reproduced in any form.

Municipality Site Plan and Development Law, Section 185(b) (Level 6)

1. Definition of Site Plan

As used in this section, the phrase "Site Plan" shall mean a drawing, sketch, or computer-generated rendering that has been prepared in order to meet the Municipality's specifications and containing all of the necessary elements that are set forth in the Municipality's applicable zoning ordinance. The required Site Plan elements which are included in the zoning ordinance may include, where appropriate, those related to parking, access, signage, landscaping, dimensions of buildings, and uses of adjacent land. The Site Plan must show the layout, arrangement, and design of the proposed use of a single parcel of land, whose parcel number is clearly indicated on said plan. Additional comments may also be included with the Site Plan, if pertinent.

2. Approval of Site Plan

(a) The Municipality may, as part of a zoning ordinance, authorize the City Council or such other appropriate administrative body to review and approve, approve with amendments, or disapprove Site Plans. The zoning ordinance itself shall legally specify the land uses that require approval of the Site Plan.

(b) When the City Council grants an authorization to approve a Site Plan pursuant to this section, the terms thereof shall condition the issuance and collection of a building permit upon said approval.

3. Restrictions Attached to the Approval of Site Plans. The City Council or such other appropriate administrative body shall have the authority to impose such reasonable restrictions that are directly related to a proposed Site Plan. Upon its approval of said Site Plan, any such Restrictions must be approved by appropriate enforcement agents or officers of the town.

4. Waiver of Requirements. The City Council or such other appropriate administrative body is further empowered, when reasonable, to waive any requirements set out above. Subject to the conditions set forth in this section, waivers must be granted prior to commencing the approval process for the site plan in the event that any such requirements are found not to be necessary in the pervasive interest of public health or safety.

© COPYRIGHT 2022. Exam SAM Study Aids & Media dba www.examsam.com
This material may not be copied or reproduced in any form.

Question 18: You work for the City Council. In the comments section, a site plan for a new grocery store states that mechanical rides for children will be provided in a corner of the store's parking lot. What should you do before proceeding to the approval process?

    A. Check whether the plan complies to all applicable zoning ordinances.

    B. Consult with an appropriate administrative body.

    C. Determine whether the site plan could be approved with amendments.

    D. Disapprove the site plan since it does not comply to the uses stated in Paragraph 1.

    E. Ensure that the rides pose no risk to public health or safety.

Question 19: According to the document, when should a building permit be obtained?

    A. When the site plan is filed.

    B. Once the site plan is approved.

    C. When the drawing, sketch, or computer-generated rendering is prepared.

    D. When compliance with any reasonable restrictions has been determined.

    E. This depends upon whether a waiver is granted.

Question 20: According to the document, which one of the following would not be a possible reason for disapproving a site plan?

    A. The plan fails to include provisions for any parking facilities.

    B. The plan includes two adjacent parcels of land.

    C. The proposed use of the land is not legally permitted.

    D. The applicant failed to collect a building permit when so notified.

    E. It has been determined that limits should be placed on certain proposals within the plan.

© COPYRIGHT 2022. Exam SAM Study Aids & Media dba www.examsam.com
This material may not be copied or reproduced in any form.

PRESS RELEASE

Work Management System (Level 7)

Our new Work Management System (WMS) provides our Company with a cloud-based, warehouse management system that reduces operating costs and administrative complexity, while promoting better scalability for both our B2C and B2B enterprises. Our WMS allows our 3PL providers, as well as our pick-pack-delivery providers, to set up their warehouses efficiently and competitively. Our WMS will therefore help our warehousers to become highly-functional distribution centers, which form the backbone of our supply chain. Regardless of the size of each warehouse, our WMS interface will allow each of our warehousers to reach their optimal performance, and therefore help our Company stay ahead of the competition.

Our WMS is more than a software application; it is delivered via a cloud-based web application, which is designed to work on desktop and laptop computers, tablets, mobile phones, and many other mobile devices. Built and designed by logistics experts and with an outstanding user experience, our new WMS mobile application interfaces with not only with computers and smartphones, but also with robotic forklifts and other PDA-controlled lifting and picking systems. With this first-class technology, we will also be able to set up records for new hires and create staff working schemes in just a few minutes, rather than in a few days as before.

Our WMS is scalable and adaptable depending on our seasonal and operational needs as it will accept anything from a hundred to hundreds of thousands of daily orders. The web-based client portal to the WMS gives us full management control, and we can report on key performance indicators and receive business intelligence that will take our business to the next level.

The integration systems which are built into the WMS enable smooth and cost-effective pairing with our ERP and business systems. Integrated with updates to our ERP, TA, and other Transport Management Systems, this innovative, technical platform will create a seamless and smooth flow for the internal

© COPYRIGHT 2022. Exam SAM Study Aids & Media dba www.examsam.com
This material may not be copied or reproduced in any form.

administrative processes of our Company, as well as creating an improved customer experience.

This WMS provides cutting-edge technology and a combination of functionalities that will allow our Company to streamline its operations. Focused on our warehousers' and customers' success and growth, our new WMS will add value and translate our investment in this new system into increased profitability.

Question 21: Based on the information in the document, which one of the following would cause problems with the functioning of the WMS?
    A. If the integration systems built into it are updated.
    B. If more warehousers are added to the system.
    C. If the number of orders it monitors suddenly increases.
    D. If it is connected to a PDA-controlled system.
    E. If the cloud in which it is based is compromised in some way.

Question 22: The 3PL providers mentioned in paragraph 1 of the document are most likely:
    A. entities that create staff working schemes.
    B. either B2C or B2B enterprises.
    C. WMS software engineers.
    D. storage or delivery providers.
    E. providers of robotic forklifts.

Question 23: Which phrase or statement from the document best supports the assertion that the WMS is scalable?
    A. "in just a few minutes, rather than in a few days"
    B. "depending on our seasonal and operational needs"
    C. "it will accept anything from a hundred to hundreds of thousands of daily orders"
    D. "the WMS gives us full management control"
    E. "The integration systems which are built into the WMS enable smooth and cost-effective pairing with our ERP and business systems."

© COPYRIGHT 2022. Exam SAM Study Aids & Media dba www.examsam.com
This material may not be copied or reproduced in any form.

U.S. Code § 1315 – Effective date of rates of duty (Level 7)

(a) ARTICLES ENTERED OR WITHDRAWN FROM WAREHOUSE FOR CONSUMPTION

Except as otherwise specially provided for, the rate or rates of duty imposed by or pursuant to this chapter or any other law on any article entered for consumption shall be the rate or rates in effect when the documents comprising the entry for consumption and any estimated or liquidated duties then required to be paid have been deposited with the Customs Service by written, electronic or such other means as the Secretary by regulation shall prescribe, except that:

(1) any article released under an informal mail entry shall be subject to duty at the rate or rates in effect when the preparation of the entry is completed;

(2) any article which is not subject to a quantitative or tariff-rate quota and which is covered by an entry for immediate transportation made at the port of original importation under section 1552 of this title, if entered for consumption at the port designated by the consignee, or his agent, in such transportation entry without having been taken into the custody of the appropriate customs officer under section 1490 of this title, shall be subject to the rate or rates in effect when the transportation entry was accepted at the port of original importation; and

(3) any article for which duties may, under section 1505 of this title, be paid at a time later than the time of making entry shall be subject to the rate or rates in effect at the time of entry.

(b) ARTICLES REMOVED FROM INTENDED PLACE OF RELEASE

Any article which has been entered for consumption but which, before release from custody of the Customs Service, is removed from the port or other place of intended release because of inaccessibility, over-carriage, strike, act of God, or unforeseen contingency, shall be subject to duty at the rate or rates in effect when the entry for consumption and any required duties were deposited in accordance with subsection (a) of this section, but only if the article is returned to such port or place within ninety days after the date of removal and the identity of the article as that covered by the entry is established in accordance with regulations prescribed by the Secretary of the Treasury.

© COPYRIGHT 2022. Exam SAM Study Aids & Media dba www.examsam.com
This material may not be copied or reproduced in any form.

Question 24: You work as a customs officer for the Customs Service. What custom rate should be paid by a shipment that arrived at the port, but then traveled back to its place of origin due to unanticipated events and will not return to the port?

    A. No payment would be owing in this instance.

    B. It would first need to be determined whether a quota applies.

    C. It would pay the rate in effect when it arrived at the port.

    D. It would pay the rate in effect when its documents were deposited.

    E. Cannot be determined from the information provided

Question 25: Section 1552, referred to in Section (a)(2) of the document, is most likely used to describe:

    A. a different type of tax that needs to be paid.

    B. a certain category of goods.

    C. a particular type of consignee or agent.

    D. the circumstances for paying duties at a later date.

    E. rules for the behavior of Customs Service officers.

Question 26: You work as a customs officer for the Customs Service. What custom rate should be paid for an article that is in port but that has not been sent by mail and that is not subject to sections 1490, 1505, or 1552 of the title mentioned in the document?

    A. the rate on the day when the goods were accepted at the port.

    B. a quantitative of tariff-rate quota.

    C. the rate on the date when the goods were removed from the Customs Service.

    D. the rate that was in effect when the paperwork for the shipment was filed.

    E. This rate may be determined at a later date.

© COPYRIGHT 2022. Exam SAM Study Aids & Media dba www.examsam.com
This material may not be copied or reproduced in any form.

Transition Payments Agreement (Level 7)

For purposes of this Agreement, the term "Transition Period" means a period of two years from the effective date of Associate's termination of employment with the Company. If the Company terminates Associate's employment, the Company will pay Associate during the Transition Period an amount equal to Associate's base salary at the rate in effect on the date of termination ("Transition Payments"). Transition Payments will commence and be paid at the end of each month.

(A) Transition Payments will not be paid if Associate is terminated as the result of Associate's violation of any Company policy.

(B) No Transition Payments will be paid if Associate voluntarily resigns or retires from employment with the Company.

(C) Given the unavailability of other programs designed to provide financial protection in such circumstances, Transition Payments will be paid under this Agreement if Associate becomes disabled. If Associate dies during the Transition Period, Associate's heirs, successors, and assignees will be entitled to the continuation of such payments.

(D) Associate's commission of any other act that is materially harmful to the Company's business interests during the Transition Period, will, at a minimum, result in the immediate termination of the Transition Payments. The Company may also pursue the recovery of the Transition Payments already made and any other legal remedies that may be available.

(E) Receipt of Transition Payments will not limit the Associate's participation during the Transition Period in any other incentive, restricted stock, performance share, stock option, stock incentive, or profit-sharing plans or programs maintained by the Company; except that Associate will not be entitled to participate in such plans or programs to the extent that the terms of said plan or program forbid participation by former associates. Such participation, if any, is non-transferrable and shall be governed by the terms of the applicable plan or program.

© COPYRIGHT 2022. Exam SAM Study Aids & Media dba www.examsam.com
This material may not be copied or reproduced in any form.

Question 27: You are an administrator of the Company's Transition Payments Agreement. You have received indisputable proof that an associate who was terminated 18 months ago is now sharing trade secrets with a competitor. What action should you take today?

    A. Terminate the associate's transition payments immediately.

    B. Inform the company's legal department to pursue legal remedies.

    C. File a claim to recover any transition payments already made.

    D. Check whether the associate participated in an incentive program.

    E. Determine whether the associate was participating in any forbidden program.

Question 28: You are an administrator of the Company's Transition Payments Agreement. An associate who quits from the Company, without giving any notice, after a heated argument with a supervisor:

    A. will only be eligible for transition payments if disabled.

    B. will not be able to transfer his or her transition payments to another party.

    C. would need to have resigned formally to be eligible for transition payments.

    D. can assign his transition payments to heirs or successors.

    E. is not eligible for transition payments.

Question 29: According to the terms of the agreement, what happens to the associate's right to participate in other plans or programs in the event of his or her death during the Transition Period?

    A. It will pass to the associate's heirs, successors, and assignees.

    B. It will be passed on only if permitted in the terms of the said plan or program.

    C. It will be passed on only if the associate was not in violation of any Company policy.

    D. It will not be passed on if the associate has committed a materially-harmful act.

    E. It will be terminated.

© COPYRIGHT 2022. Exam SAM Study Aids & Media dba www.examsam.com
This material may not be copied or reproduced in any form.

Employee Vacation Day Policy (Level 7)

1. Eligibility for Paid Vacation Days.

    1.1 Vacation days are available to employees in accordance with the Company's vacation accrual schedule.

    1.2 Employees become eligible for vacation days after one complete month of continuous service.

2. Use of Benefits.

    2.1 All vacation time must be requested in advance and approved by filing HRVT (Version 3) with the Human Resources (HR) Manager. When requesting vacation days, employees should consider department workloads by first speaking to their Department Manager.

    2.2 Employees may not use unearned vacation days, in other words, vacation days that are anticipated to be accrued in the future.

    2.3 Employees who are called into work for an emergency on a scheduled vacation day will be allowed to reschedule that vacation day.

    2.4 The maximum number of vacation hours permitted to be accumulated is 120 hours (15 days) during the first 5 continuous years of employment and thereafter. Vacation accruals increase to a maximum of 240 hours (30 days) after the employee's 10-year anniversary of continuous employment. Once employees have accumulated the maximum number of vacation hours, vacation hours will stop accruing, and any unused vacation hours beyond the aforementioned periods will be forfeited.

        2.4.1 Continuous years of employment start to be counted on the date when an employee is first classified as a part-time benefited employee or as a full-time benefited employee.

        2.4.2 Vacation accrual is calculated and updated on the employee's record at the end of each calendar month.

        2.4.3 Eligible employees may accrue vacation hours until they reach the maximum amount allowed in Section 2.4 above.

    2.5 Any employee who is not eligible for vacation pay is required to take a deduction in salary when absent from work for a full eight-hour day. This time off must be approved in advance by the employee's Department Manager. Any employee who is not eligible for vacation pay who wishes to take less than a whole day (8 hours) off will be required to work additional hours in order to make up for the time off.

3. Pay for Unused Vacation Days. All earned but unused vacation hours shall be paid to the employee at the time of separation of employment.

© COPYRIGHT 2022. Exam SAM Study Aids & Media dba www.examsam.com
This material may not be copied or reproduced in any form.

4. Holidays During Vacation. A Company holiday that falls during a scheduled vacation will not be counted as a vacation day.

5. Any vacation day requests that fall outside of the situations enumerated in this policy shall be referred to a superior of the HR Manager in the HR Department, pending his or her discretionary decision on the matter.

Question 30: Based on the document shown, the primary purpose of these rules is most likely to:

    A. explain what employees need to do when taking a day off work.

    B. inform employees about changes to the Company's vacation day policy, particularly when they terminate their employment.

    C. clarify how vacation days are to be used and accrued.

    D. enumerate the particular instances regarding when an employee is not eligible for vacation pay.

    E. advise employees against taking time off without the approval of the HR Manager.

Question 31: You are an HR manager for the Company. A part-time benefited employee who has worked for the company for 7 years has come to you, stating that he should have 260 accrued vacation hours. How should you respond to this employee?

    A. Part-time employees are not eligible for vacation days under this policy.

    B. He needs to work for the company for 3 more years in order to be able to accrue that many vacation hours.

    C. The highest number of vacation days that he can accrue is 30 days.

    D. The greatest number of vacation hours that he can accrue is 120 hours.

    E. He needs to speak with the HR manager in order for his extra hours not to be lost.

Question 32: You are an HR manager for the Company. An employee has requested to reschedule her entire week of vacation after having been called back into work on an emergency on the first day that she was away. What should you tell her?

    A. She will be allowed to reschedule only one vacation day.

    B. She will have to wait until the end of the month for the update.

    C. She will forfeit one day of vacation pay if she decides to do this.

    D. This would be allowed only if a Company holiday falls within the rescheduled vacation days.

    E. Her request needs to be decided upon by a boss of the HR Manager.

© COPYRIGHT 2022. Exam SAM Study Aids & Media dba www.examsam.com
This material may not be copied or reproduced in any form.

Continuing Education Bylaws for State Certified Accountants (Level 7)

Acceptable formal continuing education for the license for the practice of accountancy in this State shall mean formal programs of learning which contribute to or help to maintain professional knowledge or practice and which meet the requirements laid out below. Accountant must earn 120 hours of continuing education credit every three years, i.e. during a triennial period. A period of 3 months grace shall be added to this period when requested.

1. Except as otherwise provided in paragraph (2) below, in order to be acceptable to this State, recognized continuing education areas of study shall consist of instruction conducted by approved sponsors in the following subjects only: accountancy, financial statement auditing, individual or business taxation, financial advisory services, consultancy service related to specialized industries, or any other types of formal programs related to the practice of accounting that may be acceptable to the State. The types of formal programs which may be accepted by the State include:

   i. any courses taken for academic credit at any fully-accredited university or college, which are reflected on an official university or college transcript, and that fall within one or more of the recognized subject areas described in Section 1 above;

   ii. other organized educational and technical programs which contribute to the growth of the professional knowledge of the Accountant and which have been pre-approved by the State prior to the Accountant participating in the program.

2. In addition to instruction taken pursuant to subdivisions 1.i and 1.ii above, the following activities may be used to meet the continuing education requirement, provided that the number of hours allowed for such activities for any Accountant does not exceed fifty percent of the total number of hours of continuing education claimed during the Accountant's license renewal period:

   i. Teaching a course at an accredited university or college, or at any other institution which has been pre-approved by the State, provided that the instruction is in one of the subject areas set forth in paragraph 1 above.

   ii. Such teaching shall not be acceptable if the Accountant has taught the course previously and is not providing updated or revised course information. The maximum amount of continuing education credit that will be awarded for

© COPYRIGHT 2022. Exam SAM Study Aids & Media dba www.examsam.com
This material may not be copied or reproduced in any form.

teaching a university or college course is 15 credit hours per academic semester or 10 credit hours per academic trimester.

3. Authoring an article in a peer-received national accountancy journal in one of the areas mentioned in paragraph 1 above shall receive 8 hours of continuing credit per article. Credit granted under this paragraph is subject to the limit of 56 hours for the triennial period.

Question 33: You work for the State. An accountant has attended two different 8-hour accountancy courses each year at a university during the past three years, but all of her other credits are for online business taxation courses. She wonders if these credit hours will be acceptable. What should you do?

A. Inquire whether her online courses were approved by the State in advance.
B. Inform her that she can write an article to make up for any missing credit hours.
C. Tell her that she has exceeded the fifty percent limit stated in Paragraph 2.
D. Ask whether she has received a transcript for the online courses.
E. Mention that one or more of her courses were not in an approved subject area.

Question 34: You work for the State. You have noticed that the accountant's continuing education form indicated that he attended a course that was not offered by an approved sponsor or accredited academic institution. What should you do?

A. Determine whether this course falls within the prescribed limits.
B. Disallow the credits and inform the accountant accordingly.
C. Tell the State to revoke the accountant's license for failure to comply with the Bylaws.
D. Inform the accountant that he can seek retroactive approval for the course during the grace period.
E. Allow the hours if they fall within the fifty percent limit.

Question 35: What is the maximum number of hours that an accountant can claim per year for writing journal articles that meet the criteria stated in this document?

A. 60
B. 56
C. 30
D. 18
E. Cannot be determined from the information provided.

© COPYRIGHT 2022. Exam SAM Study Aids & Media dba www.examsam.com
This material may not be copied or reproduced in any form.

WORKKEYS WORKPLACE DOCUMENTS PRACTICE TEST 2

Instructions: Read each of the passages below and then answer the questions that follow each one. Select only ONE answer per question. There is no penalty for incorrect answers, so you should guess an answer choice even when you are unsure. You are allowed 55 minutes to answer all 35 questions.

Email Response (Level 3)

Dear Jonas,

Thank you so much for your assistance during our recent software update. You and your staff really came through for us. This truly proves what it means to go the extra mile.

I want to personally thank you for all the extra effort you put in. Next week, please plan a day to take yourself and your staff to lunch at the Ivy Restaurant. The meal will on the company account, to thank everyone for all of their hard work.

Please submit the receipt for the meal to Fatima in HR. Any other expenses should be submitted on your personal expense reimbursement form, as usual.

Regards,

Rachel

© COPYRIGHT 2022. Exam SAM Study Aids & Media dba www.examsam.com
This material may not be copied or reproduced in any form.

Question 1: What is the primary purpose of the document?

    A. to thank employees for their hard work

    B. to communicate a policy update to the software department

    C. to inform Jonas to treat staff on the software update team to a meal out

    D. to tell staff that they performed well on the recent project

    E. to set down new policies for staff lunches

Question 2: According to the document, what should Jonas do after the meal?

    A. inform Fatima that the event has taken place

    B. provide proof of the expense from the restaurant to a representative in HR

    C. submit it on his personal expense form

    D. treat it as usual, like any other expense

    E. thank his staff for their hard work

© COPYRIGHT 2022. Exam SAM Study Aids & Media dba www.examsam.com
This material may not be copied or reproduced in any form.

Customer Refund Policy (Level 4)

Van Winkle Returns Policy

You do not have to refund a customer if they:

- knew an item was defective when they bought it

- damaged an item by trying to repair it themselves or by getting someone else to do it

- no longer want an item (unless they bought it without seeing it)

You must offer a refund for the following items, but only if they are defective:

- personalized items and custom-made items, like customized clothing and curtains

- perishable items, like frozen food or flowers

- swimwear and intimate apparel

- any other item that is unboxed or unwrapped

© COPYRIGHT 2022. Exam SAM Study Aids & Media dba www.examsam.com
This material may not be copied or reproduced in any form.

Question 3: You work for Van Winkle. A customer did not see merchandise before purchasing it. What should you do if the customer asks for a refund?

    A. grant a refund for the item if they do not wish to keep it

    B. ask them if the item is defective

    C. ask if they tried to repair the item themselves

    D. ask if someone else tried to repair the item

    E. inform them that a refund will not be granted in this case

Question 4: You work for Van Winkle. A customer wants to return an item that is out of its original box. According to the document, what should you do?

    A. ask the customer whether they have the original packaging

    B. investigate whether the item has been personalized in some way

    C. determine whether the item has a flaw or fault

    D. grant the customer an immediate refund

    E. deny the refund request

© COPYRIGHT 2022. Exam SAM Study Aids & Media dba www.examsam.com
This material may not be copied or reproduced in any form.

Issuance of Replacement Employee ID Cards (Level 4)

If you lose or damage your employee ID card, you will need to pay $40 for each replacement. You need to provide a clear photograph of your face to have your card reissued. You also need to have a status of "good standing" with the company. To check your status, log on to the company website.

As a result of our new computer system, any new cards will have a new employee number with 15 digits. Any cards issued prior to January 1 will have 12-digit ID numbers. It will take at least two weeks to update your details on the company's computer system.

Question 5: You need a new ID card after January 1. Which one of the following will you not necessarily need to do?
   A. pay the $40 fee
   B. provide a picture of yourself
   C. have the correct status
   D. wait two weeks or more for the system to update your information
   E. log on to the company's website

Question 6: Which one of the following statements is true regarding employee ID cards issued before January 1.
   A. They were re-issued for free.
   B. They did not have photographs.
   C. The employee ID number on them had 15 digits.
   D. The employee ID number on them had 12 numbers.
   E. The employee did not have two wait two weeks to receive them.

© COPYRIGHT 2022. Exam SAM Study Aids & Media dba www.examsam.com
This material may not be copied or reproduced in any form.

Introduction and Fundraising Drive Letter (Level 5)

First of all, we would like to introduce ourselves. Love Outdoors is the best sportswear store in our county. We sell high-quality sports and casual wear clothing at reasonable prices. If you don't know us already, we encourage you to visit us and see our top-notch merchandise for yourself.

We would also like to tell you about our participation in this year's fundraising drive for the American Cancer Society. Engaging in essential and timely research, the American Cancer Society is one of the most important eleemosynary organizations in our nation. To assist with this year's fundraising drive for the charity, Love Outdoors has agreed to donate 25 percent of every sale during the month of June to the American Cancer Society. We are proud to join in the fight against cancer, and we sincerely hope that you will visit us this June to take the opportunity to contribute to a good cause, as well as take home some new clothes.

Question 7: Which one of the following is the closest to the meaning of the word "eleemosynary" as it is used in the document?
   A. scientific
   B. financial
   C. charitable
   D. hierarchical
   E. well-known

Question 8: You work as a financial manager for Love Outdoors. What do you most likely regard as your most important activity this June?
   A. to increase positivity within the local community
   B. to set a precedent for fundraising that other companies should follow
   C. to assist the American Cancer Drive in meeting its goals
   D. to drive more sales to the store via the fundraising campaign
   E. to ensure that good quality, affordable clothing is delivered to your store

© COPYRIGHT 2022. Exam SAM Study Aids & Media dba www.examsam.com
This material may not be copied or reproduced in any form.

Management of Forest Lands Subsidy [MFLS] (Level 5)

This law encourages the effective management of private forest lands and sound forestry practices for future forest crop production. It balances the objectives of individual property owners against those of recreational users, wildlife habitats, and protection of the natural water table. Any owner of more than 10 continuous acres of non-commercial forest land in any town or city may apply for the subsidy.

Owners of forest lands may elect to designate the entire forest area as open to public access for purposes of activities such as hiking, dog walking, hunting, fishing, and cross-country skiing. The landowner can also elect to designate a specific area within a forested parcel of land to be closed to public access.

The following fields of the MFLS application form should be completed:

Fields 1 to 3 – Enter acres (1), school district code (2), and assessed value (3) for each parcel of land.

Field 4 – Identify the acreages to be designated as "Open." These acreages shall be taxed at $5.50 per acre.

Field 5 – Identify the acreages to be designated as "Closed." These acreages shall be taxed at $12.75 per acre. This includes acreages that are designated as closed due to public health and safety concerns.

© COPYRIGHT 2022. Exam SAM Study Aids & Media dba www.examsam.com
This material may not be copied or reproduced in any form.

Question 9: According to document, in order to apply for the MFLS, an applicant needs to:

    A. indicate that they will place their entire forest area in the program.

    B. explain which activities will be conducted on the land.

    C. pay tax at $5.50 per acre.

    D. pay tax at $12.75 per acre.

    E. own more than ten acres of the appropriate kind of land.

Question 10: It is your job to check all incoming MFLS application forms. An application has just come in from a business that is requesting a subsidy for twenty contiguous acres of land behind their hotel complex. What should you do?

    A. Determine whether fields 1 to 5 of the form have been filed in.

    B. Advise the applicant that the subsidy is for non-business land owners only.

    C. Check to see whether the business is up-to-date with their tax payments.

    D. Ask the applicant whether the land will be used for any recreational purpose.

    E. Investigate whether any wildlife habitats will be affected.

© COPYRIGHT 2022. Exam SAM Study Aids & Media dba www.examsam.com
This material may not be copied or reproduced in any form.

Contract for Services Rendered (Level 6)

This is a contract entered into by Office Supply Services (hereinafter referred to as "the Provider") and ABC Incorporated (hereinafter referred to as "the Client") on the date indicated by the signatures to this document.

The Client hereby engages the Provider to provide services described herein under the "Services to Be Rendered by Provider" section below. The Provider hereby agrees to provide the Client with such services in exchange for the consideration described herein under the "Payment for Services Rendered" section below.

Services to Be Rendered by Provider:

1. To supply the Client with requested office and paper products, including but not limited to printing paper, paper towels, paper folders, pens, paperclips, and envelopes.

2. To deliver said products to the Client within five business day of receiving an order.

3. To ensure that the Provider's website and device application are functional and available to the client.

4. To accept returns from the Client for a full refund if received by the Provider within one week after delivery to the Client.

Payment for Services Rendered:

The Client shall pay the Provider for services rendered according to the Payment Schedule attached, within 7 calendar days of the date on any invoice for products supplied by the Provider. Should the Client fail to pay the Provider the full amount specified in any invoice within 7 calendar days of the invoice's date, a late fee equal to $35 shall be added to the amount due and interest of 12 percent per annum shall accrue from the calendar day following the invoice's date.

This agreement shall not become binding upon any party until both parties have agreed to it. Amendments to this agreement can be made in writing by

© COPYRIGHT 2022. Exam SAM Study Aids & Media dba www.examsam.com
This material may not be copied or reproduced in any form.

agreement of both of the parties. The agreement may not be assigned or transferred to any third party. Neither party shall be liable to perform their obligations under this contract where such failure or delay is beyond the reasonable control of the parties.

Question 11: You work for Office Supply Services. A client has called you, wanting an explanation for an additional $45 charge on a $1,000 invoice that was due a month ago. What should you tell the client?

    A. There is a penalty for paying late.

    B. All invoices need to be paid within 7 days of receipt.

    C. Partial payments of invoices will not be accepted.

    D. $35 was added for late payment and $10 was added for interest.

    E. The client's signature on the bottom of the invoice indicates their agreement to the extra charges.

Question 12: Based on the agreement shown, what will happen if the client goes out of business?

    A. The agreement will be void.

    B. The agreement will be handed over to another party.

    C. The Provider must be informed of this in writing.

    D. The Client will not be required to make further payments.

    E. The Client will remain liable for timely payment of any outstanding invoices.

© COPYRIGHT 2022. Exam SAM Study Aids & Media dba www.examsam.com
This material may not be copied or reproduced in any form.

Data Protection Policy (Level 6)

Policy Purpose

Our Data Protection Policy shows our commitment to treating the information we receive from our employees, customers, and other interested parties with the utmost confidentiality and with respect towards individual rights.

Scope

This policy refers to all parties who provide any amount of information to us.

Who is covered under the Data Protection Policy?

The personal data of the employees of our company and its subsidiaries are covered by this policy. Our policy also covers the data of anyone we collaborate with or who acts on our behalf.

Policy Elements

We occasionally need to obtain and process personal data as part of our operations. This information includes any data that can be used to identify a person, including names, addresses, digital footprints and photographs, tax identification numbers, and financial information.

Our company collects this data transparently, with the full knowledge and cooperation of all parties concerned. Once this information is available to us, the following rules apply.

Our data will be kept accurate and up-to-date; collected lawfully and fairly; stored and used by the company in accordance with all applicable laws; and protected against unauthorized access by any parties, whether they be internal or external to the company.

Our data will not be communicated informally; stored for more than seven years; transferred to any other organizations; or distributed to any third party, other than the ones agreed upon by the data's owner and requests from law enforcement authorities.

© COPYRIGHT 2022. Exam SAM Study Aids & Media dba www.examsam.com
This material may not be copied or reproduced in any form.

Actions

In order to improve our data protection procedures, we're committed to monitoring access to data; creating new, more effective data collection procedures; instructing employees about online privacy; building computer networks with increased security; and establishing data protection practices such as access authorization, data encryption, frequent data backups, and document shredding.

Question 13: A independent contractor has discovered a copy of their invoice to the company freely available on the internet, clearly displaying the contractor's personal details and tax ID number, and has called you to complain. How should you respond?

    A. Inform the caller that independent contractors are not covered by the policy.

    B. Check to see whether information on the invoice is up-to-date.

    C. Tell him that the data was stored in conformity with all applicable laws.

    D. Apologize to him for the error and try to get the invoice taken down.

    E. Advise him that access to the information is lawful since it is external to the company.

Question 14: Which of the following can be inferred from the "Actions" section of the document?

    A. The company's current computer system is very poor.

    B. The company regards their data protection procedures as something that can be constantly improved.

    C. The company has discovered that new employees are often unaware of how to achieve online privacy.

    D. The company's current data collection procedures are regarded as antiquated.

    E. The company's data collection procedures rely on access authorization at the present time.

© COPYRIGHT 2022. Exam SAM Study Aids & Media dba www.examsam.com
This material may not be copied or reproduced in any form.

Hazardous Materials Handling Procedures (Level 6)

The following are ten basic rules that we expect all of our employees who handle or work around hazardous materials always to know and follow:

1. Follow all established procedures and perform job duties in the manner in which you have been instructed.

2. Think ahead and be cautious. Think about what potential problems lay ahead and pay close attention to all procedures while working with or around hazardous substances.

3. Use Personal Protective Equipment (PPE). Inspect PPE carefully before each use to make sure it is fully functional and safe to use. Replace PPE that has been worn for more than 8 hours since overly-used PPE will not provide adequate protection.

4. Make sure all hazardous materials are properly labeled and stored. Never use any chemical that has not been stored or labeled properly. Report damaged or illegible labels to your Department Manager immediately.

5. Use any hazardous material only for its intended purpose. For example, never use solvents to cleanse your hands, regardless of how soiled they are.

6. Employees handling hazardous materials need to read labels on all chemicals before they use or handle them. This information can be found on the applicable Safety Data Sheet (SDS), which explains how to deal with handling and storing materials, as well as with cleaning up spills and providing relevant first-aid when necessary.

7. Never eat or drink during the handing of hazardous substances. Always wear gloves while handing hazardous substances, and remove your gloves and wash your hands thoroughly when the handling procedure has concluded.

© COPYRIGHT 2022. Exam SAM Study Aids & Media dba www.examsam.com
This material may not be copied or reproduced in any form.

8. Know emergency procedures and the location of emergency equipment. This means knowing evacuation procedures, emergency reporting, and dealing with spills, leaks, or fires and understanding employee decontamination procedures.

9. Keep the work area immaculately clean. Clean work surfaces at least once per shift in order to minimize contamination risks.

10. Also keep emergency shower and eyewash stations impeccably clean. Never allow clutter to build up around these stations.

Question 15: What is the most likely rationale behind the issuance of this document?
   A. to advise employees to be vigilant when using dangerous substances
   B. to warn employees about using chemicals that are not labeled
   C. to conform to what is required for the company's business insurance
   D. to remind employees about important emergency procedures
   E. to clarify the correct use of company PPE

Question 16: You are an employee for the company. You need to use a chemical that is in a bottle, but you are not able to find its SDS. What should you do first?
   A. Be sure to know the first-aid procedures before handling it.
   B. Do not use the substance for any purpose besides its designated one.
   C. Report it to your Department Manager as soon as you can.
   D. Use extra non-previously-worn PPE when handling it.
   E. Check to see whether information about the substance can be found on the label of the container.

Question 17: You are an employee for the company. What action should you always undertake first when you are finished using a hazardous substance?
   A. wash your hands thoroughly
   B. check whether any of the substance has leaked out or spilled during use
   C. take off protective hand coverings
   D. clean your work surfaces
   E. take a shower

© COPYRIGHT 2022. Exam SAM Study Aids & Media dba www.examsam.com
This material may not be copied or reproduced in any form.

To: All Financial Advisors with L & M Investments (Level 6)

Note that you must advise clients of the potential risk considerations enumerated in this email before they make any investment with us.

1. An investment in this fund is not managed by us and should be made with an understanding of the risks involved in an investment in a portfolio of corporate bonds and common stocks.

2. Common stocks are subject to certain risks, such as an economic recession and the possible deterioration of either the financial condition of the company issuing the stocks or the general condition of the stock market.

3. A corporate bond ("bond") is a type of loan taken out by companies. In effect, investors lend a company money when they buy its bonds. In exchange, the company pays interest and returns the amount invested on the redemption date.

4. The value of bonds can vary significantly based on the terms of the bond's indenture, a legal document that outlines the characteristics of the bond. Because each bond issue is different, it is important to explain the precise terms to clients before they invest.

5. A bond can be secured or unsecured. Unsecured bonds are called debentures; their interest payments and return of the principal are guaranteed only by the issuing company. If the company fails, a client may get little of his or her principal back.

6. On the other hand, a secured bond is an investment in which specific assets are pledged to bond holders if the company cannot repay the debt.

7. A company has the right to pay off any bond early, meaning that investors may not get the return on the investment that they had expected.

© COPYRIGHT 2022. Exam SAM Study Aids & Media dba www.examsam.com
This material may not be copied or reproduced in any form.

8. When a company goes bankrupt, it pays money back to investors in a particular order as it liquidates. After a company has sold off all its assets, it will pay off its debts, including bonds, first. Owners of stock get the remainder. For this reason, most clients believe that bonds are more financially secure than stocks.

Question 18: What is the most likely rationale behind sections 1 and 2 of the document?

    A. to state that advisors must inform clients that L & M has no liability for investors' losses

    B. to explain the risks of investing to L & M staff

    C. to clarify the general condition of the stock market to L & M staff

    D. to point out to staff that the fund is not managed

    E. to mention to advisors that they should apprise clients about the possibility of recession

Question 19: You are an investor with L & M. You have purchased a secured corporate bond, but have discovered that the company that you invested in has gone bankrupt. Are you likely to get back your money on the investment?

    A. No, because the investment is classified as a debenture.

    B. No, due to the fact that you were advised about the risks of investing beforehand.

    C. No, since no assets have been pledged to bond holders.

    D. Yes, provided that the company you invested in has made money on the sale of its assets.

    E. Yes, as long as the stock market is stable.

Question 20: Based on the information in the document, under what conditions would a client earn the most money from a portfolio investment in corporate bonds?

    A. When the portfolio is managed independently

    B. When the bonds are secured

    C. When the bonds are indentured

    D. When the bonds are held until the redemption date

    E. When the economy is functioning well

© COPYRIGHT 2022. Exam SAM Study Aids & Media dba www.examsam.com
This material may not be copied or reproduced in any form.

Company Paid Sick Leave Policy (Level 7)

The Company's paid sick leave policy permits employees to take sick leave to attend to their own health conditions, as well as allowing leave to care for a member of the employee's immediate family. "Family member" is defined as a spouse, child, sibling, parent, grandparent, parent-in-law, or grandchild. Health conditions covered include both physical and mental health issues. Employees may also use sick leave to recover when they or a family member are the victim of any physical attack, public or domestic assault, or stalking.

Paid sick leave accrues to any employee who has worked for the Company for at least 30 days as a full-time employee or 60 days as a part-time employee. An employee classification as part-time or full-time is indicated both on the employee's initial written offer of employment, as well as on each monthly pay receipt. Part-time employees can begin using accrued sick leave when they have worked for the Company for 90 days, and full-time employees can begin using their accrued sick pay after 45 days of work. All of those working for the Company as independent contractors or private consultants are not classified as employees of the Company, and are therefore not eligible for paid sick leave under this policy or under any other Company policy.

One hour of paid sick leave is accrued for every 10 hours worked and is recorded on the employee's HRR-12. An employee may carry over paid sick leave from year to year, but the carryover is capped at a maximum of 5 days of paid sick leave carryover in total.

Employees who experience no illnesses during a particular calendar year are requested to use 3 days of paid sick leave as personal days in the following calendar year in order to avoid the administrative burden of calculating paid sick leave carryover amounts. These 3 personal days should be taken from January 1 to January 31 of the following calendar year. The employee must prepare PSPL-5, which must be approved by their department manager.

The Company does not pay out accrued sick leave when an employee leaves the company, whether the leave be of the employee's volition or at the Company's request. However, if an employee leaves the Company and is re-hired within three months, their accrued sick leave days at the time of leaving will be reinstated.

© COPYRIGHT 2022. Exam SAM Study Aids & Media dba www.examsam.com
This material may not be copied or reproduced in any form.

Question 21: What happens if an employee takes no days of paid sick leave during the year?

  A. They will forfeit all of the sick leave they earned during the year.

  B. They will be able to carryforward five sick days to next year.

  C. They will need to prepare HRR-12 to report this.

  D. They may be eligible to use 3 of those days as personal days next year.

  E. It depends on whether they are part-time or full-time.

Question 22: Which of the following is the most likely purpose of the PSPL-5?

  A. to record accrued paid sick leave

  B. to approve paid sick leave

  C. to pay out accrued sick leave for terminated employees

  D. to provide the manager with a record of an employee's personal days

  E. to request a specific type of time off

Question 23: You work as an administrator of the Paid Sick Leave Policy for the company. A part-time employee contacts you, stating that she would like to use some of her sick days for her husband's upcoming operation. She has worked for the company for 15 weeks. How should you respond?

  A. Tell her that employees are only allowed paid sick leave when undergoing surgery themselves.

  B. Ask her what dates the operation is to determine if she allowed paid sick leave.

  C. Inform her that she has not worked long enough to accrue sick pay.

  D. Advise her that she is allowed paid sick leave after 45 days of work.

  E. Ask her to bring in her latest monthly pay receipt.

© COPYRIGHT 2022. Exam SAM Study Aids & Media dba www.examsam.com
This material may not be copied or reproduced in any form.

SPECIAL PACKAGING INSTRUCTIONS (Level 7)

15 USC Sec 1471-1477 [Public Law]

SEC. 3. [15 U.S.C. § 1472]

(a) The Consumer Product Safety Commission may establish in accordance with the provisions of this Act, by regulation, standards for the special packaging of any household substance if it finds that—

   (1) the degree or nature of the hazard to children in the availability of such substance, by reason of its packaging, is such that special packaging is required to protect children from serious personal injury or serious illness resulting from handling, using, or ingesting such substance; and (2) the special packaging to be required by such standard is technically feasible, practicable, and appropriate for such substance.

(b) In establishing a standard under this section, the Commission shall consider—

   (1) the reasonableness of such standard; (2) available scientific, medical, and engineering data concerning special packaging and concerning childhood accidental ingestions, illness, and injury caused by household substances; (3) the manufacturing practices of industries affected by this Act; and (4) the nature and use of the household substance.

(c) In carrying out this Act, the Commission shall publish its findings, its reasons therefore, and citation of the sections of statutes which authorize its action.

(d) Nothing in this Act shall authorize the Commission to prescribe specific packaging designs, product content, package quantity, or, with the exception of authority granted in section 4(a)(2) of this Act [15 U.S.C. § 1473(a)(2)] for labeling. In the case of a household substance for which special packaging is required pursuant to a regulation under this section, the Commission may in such regulation prohibit the packaging of such substance in packages which it determines are unnecessarily attractive to children.

(e) Nothing in this Act shall be construed to require the Commission, in establishing a standard under this section, to prepare a comparison of the costs that would be incurred in complying with such standard with the benefits of such standard.

CONVENTIONAL PACKAGES, MARKETING

SEC. 4. [15 U.S.C. § 1473]

(a) For the purpose of making any household substance which is subject to a standard established under section 3 readily available to elderly or handicapped

© COPYRIGHT 2022. Exam SAM Study Aids & Media dba www.examsam.com
This material may not be copied or reproduced in any form.

persons unable to use such substance when packaged in compliance with such standard, the manufacturer or packer, as the case may be, may package any household substance, subject to such a standard, in packaging of a single size which does not comply with such standard if [. . . the package] bears conspicuous labeling stating: "This package is for households without young children"; except that the Commission may by regulation prescribe a substitute statement to the same effect for packaging too small to accommodate such labeling.

Question 24: You work for the Commission that creates the special packaging instructions. In terms of deciding whether a special packaging standard is reasonable, you do not need to:
    A. consider the costs in implementing such a standard.
    B. determine whether the packaging is enticing to children.
    C. compare it to resent research on accidents of children consuming dangerous substances.
    D. look at how factories produce the product.
    E. evaluate the labeling of the product.

Question 25: You work for the Commission, enforcing the special packaging instructions. You have discovered that a major manufacturer of a household substance is selling it in special packaging, marketed as "easy opening" for those with arthritis. What should you do?
    A. Determine whether the product has recently been ingested by children.
    B. Investigate whether the product has appropriate labeling.
    C. Evaluate whether the special packaging is in compliance with the standards of the manufacturer.
    D. Assess the impact of this variance on other manufacturers.
    E. Prohibit the packaging of the product in this manner.

Question 26: The most likely purpose of these two sections of the law is to:
    A. ensure that any danger posed by the packaging of harmful substances is reasonably reduced.
    B. balance the needs of children against those of the elderly.
    C. prohibit marketing which is attractive to children.
    D. advise manufacturers about appropriate packaging designs.
    E. lay out the circumstances when special labeling is not required.

© COPYRIGHT 2022. Exam SAM Study Aids & Media dba www.examsam.com
This material may not be copied or reproduced in any form.

Non-Disclosure Agreement (Level 7)

This agreement is for the purpose of preventing the unauthorized disclosure of Confidential Information as defined in Section 1 below. Upon signing this Agreement, the parties are entering into a confidential relationship relating to the non-disclosure of confidential information, as well as certain proprietary and business information ("Confidential Information").

1. **Definition of Confidential Information**. "Confidential Information" under this Agreement includes any and all material or information that has or could have monetary value in any venture or commercial value in the business in which the Disclosing Party is engaged. When the Confidential Information is written in form, the Disclosing Party must label or stamp the materials in red with the word "Confidential" clearly displaying on the face of the applicable documents. When Confidential Information is transmitted orally, the Disclosing Party must, after such oral disclosure, promptly provide a written statement to the Receiving Party indicating that said oral communication constitutes Confidential Information.

2. **Exclusions from Confidential Information**. The obligations of the Receiving Party under this Agreement shall exclude information that is: (a) publicly well-known at the time of disclosure or which thereafter becomes publicly well-known by no action of the Receiving Party; (b) discovered by the Receiving Party through legitimate means other than from the Disclosing Party or Disclosing Party's agents or representatives; (c) disclosed by the Receiving Party with prior written approval from the Disclosing Party; or (d) that has been created by the Receiving Party on behalf of the Disclosing Party.

3. **Obligations of Receiving Party**. Receiving Party shall hold in the strictest confidence the Confidential Information for the sole and exclusive benefit of the Disclosing Party. Receiving Party shall carefully restrict access to Confidential Information by employees, contractors, and third parties as is reasonably required and shall require those persons to sign nondisclosure restrictions when applicable under this Agreement.

4. **Time Periods**. The nondisclosure provisions of this Agreement shall extend beyond the termination of this Agreement; Receiving Party's obligation to hold Confidential Information in confidence shall remain in effect until the Confidential Information no longer qualifies as a trade secret as defined by the USPTO.

© COPYRIGHT 2022. Exam SAM Study Aids & Media dba www.examsam.com
This material may not be copied or reproduced in any form.

Question 27: You work for the business to which the non-disclosure agreement applies. You have just told a client about a new product. You do not want the client to share the information with anyone else. What should you do?

    A. Stamp the word "Confidential" on the appropriate form.

    B. Tell the client that the information is confidential.

    C. Write to the client to inform them that the information is confidential.

    D. Determine whether the information has become publicly well-known.

    E. Ensure that any further access to the information is restricted.

Question 28: You work for the business to which the non-disclosure agreement applies. You have discovered that someone who works on a casual basis for the company has posted the details of one of the company's new designs online. What should you do?

    A. Evaluate the monetary amount of the commercial value of the design.

    B. Investigate whether the person was engaged as a contractor.

    C. Determine whether the information was received in a legitimate manner.

    D. Look into whether the information was transmitted by company email.

    E. No action can be taken for information shared by non-employees.

Question 29: As mentioned in section 4, the USTPO is most likely to be:

    A. a particular category of non-disclosure agreements

    B. a certain type of "Receiving Party"

    C. an obligation to regard information as confidential

    D. an organization that deals with trade secrets

    E. a restriction on non-disclosure agreements

© COPYRIGHT 2022. Exam SAM Study Aids & Media dba www.examsam.com
This material may not be copied or reproduced in any form.

Letter of Intent (Level 7)

This Letter of Intent ("LOI") sets forth certain Binding Provisions between Buyer and Seller with respect to the possible acquisition of commercial real estate commonly known as ("Premises"). This LOI will remain open for contractual execution by the other party for six months after the date indicated in Paragraph D. However, the party submitting this LOI may withdraw this LOI in writing at any time prior to the other party's execution.

Upon execution by Buyer and Seller of this LOI, the following lettered paragraphs (collectively, "Binding Provisions") will constitute the legally binding and enforceable agreement of Buyer and Seller.

A. Reasonable Efforts. Buyer and Seller shall, in good faith, negotiate and use reasonable efforts to arrive at a mutually acceptable Contract for execution on or before the termination date set forth in Paragraph D (ii) below.

B. Exclusive Dealings. Until the Contract has been duly executed and delivered by all the parties or until the Binding Provisions have been terminated pursuant to Paragraph D below, whichever occurs sooner: (i) Seller will not enter into any negotiations or agreements with any other Person or entity for the purpose of selling or exchanging the Premises; and (ii) Buyer will not enter into any negotiations or agreements for the purpose of buying or exchanging any real property, other than the Premises, to be used by Buyer for the purpose for which Buyer seeks to purchase the Premises.

C. Costs. Buyer and Seller shall each bear all of their own respective costs and expenses, including expenses of their legal counsels, representatives, and other advisors incurred at any time in connection with this LOI. No maximum limit shall be placed upon these costs as each party shall retain responsibility for their own potential expenditures under this Contact.

D. Termination. The Binding Provisions of this LOI may be terminated: (i) at any time by mutual written consent of Buyer and Seller; or (ii) upon written notice by any party to the other by December 21, 2022; provided, however, that the termination of the Binding Provisions due to a breach of the terms of the LOI by either party shall not affect the liability of a party for breach of any of said Binding Provisions.

© COPYRIGHT 2022. Exam SAM Study Aids & Media dba www.examsam.com
This material may not be copied or reproduced in any form.

Question 30: What explanation best describes the phrase "remain open for contractual execution" from paragraph 1?
  A. That the LOI will be legally-binding if signed before June 21, 2023.
  B. That commercial real estate must be operating as a business enterprise
  C. That the parties must agree to the applicable parts of the letter
  D. That the parties must act with reasonable efforts and good faith
  E. That the purpose of the LOI must remain unchanged

Question 31: According to the document, which one of the following would be an acceptable reason for terminating the LOI?
  A. The buyer is considering changing the purpose of the premises.
  B. The seller is selling a similar type of premises to another buyer.
  C. The buyer verbally tells the seller that they no longer want the premises.
  D. The buyer has breached the terms of the LOI.
  E. The costs under the LOI have exceeded the maximum amount.

Question 32: You are the Seller in the executed LOI. You have found out that the Buyer is looking at purchasing a grocery store from another party, in addition to the motel they are purchasing from you. What should you do?
  A. Ascertain whether 180 days have elapsed.
  B. Alter the "Exclusive Dealings" clause of the LOI.
  C. Determine whether the Buyer is bearing all applicable costs under the LOI.
  D. Terminate the LOI in writing with immediate effect.
  E. Take no action.

© COPYRIGHT 2022. Exam SAM Study Aids & Media dba www.examsam.com
This material may not be copied or reproduced in any form.

Public Law Statute 77 – Uniform Commercial Code (Level 7)

PART 2—FORM, FORMATION AND READJUSTMENT OF CONTRACT
§28:2—201.

Formal requirements; statute of frauds:

(1) Except as otherwise provided in this section, a contract for the sale of goods for the price of $500 or more is not enforceable by way of action or defense unless there is some writing sufficient to indicate that a contract for sale has been made between the parties and signed by the party against whom enforcement is sought or by their authorized agent or broker. A writing is not insufficient because it omits or incorrectly states a term agreed upon, but the contract is not enforceable under this paragraph beyond the quantity of goods shown in such writing.

(2) Between merchants, if within a reasonable time a writing in confirmation of the contract and sufficient against the sender is received, and the party receiving it has reason to know its contents, it satisfies the requirements of subsection (1) against such party unless written notice of objection to its contents is given within ten days after it is received.

(3) A contract which does not satisfy the requirements of subsection (1) but which is valid in other respects is enforceable

(a) if the goods are to be specially manufactured for the buyer and are not suitable for sale to others in the ordinary course of the seller's business and the seller, before notice of repudiation is received and under circumstances which reasonably indicate that the goods are for the buyer, has made either a substantial beginning of their manufacture or commitments for their procurement; or (b) if the party against whom enforcement is sought admits in their pleading, testimony, or otherwise in court that a contract for sale was made, but the contract is not enforceable under this provision beyond the quantity of goods admitted; or (c) with respect to goods for which payment has been made and accepted or which have been received and accepted (section 28:2—606).

© COPYRIGHT 2022. Exam SAM Study Aids & Media dba www.examsam.com
This material may not be copied or reproduced in any form.

Question 33: You are a merchant. A customer wishes to object to part of a contract for $1,000 worth of goods from you that they signed 5 weeks ago. What action should you take?

    A. Investigate whether the contract has been previously altered.

    B. Refute the objection since too much time has elapsed.

    C. Look into whether an agent signed the contract on behalf of the customer.

    D. Ascertain whether any terms of the contract were stated incorrectly.

    E. Determine whether the customer has any other action or defense.

Question 34: You own a factory. You are nearly finished manufacturing a special order for a contract of customer of goods that cannot otherwise be sold on the open market. The customer tells you that they want to cancel the order. How to you respond?

    A. Tell the customer that you need the request in writing.

    B. Investigate whether any pre-payments have been made on the order.

    C. Inform the customer that the order may not be canceled.

    D. Determine whether section 28:2—606 applies to this case.

    E. Cancel the order with immediate effect.

Question 35: You have entered into a sales contract with a buyer of goods priced at $550. You have noticed that the customer's last name is misspelled. Is the contract valid?

    A. Yes, the contract will not be considered insufficient.

    B. No, further written notice needs to be provided to the customer.

    C. No, because the value of goods is not high enough.

    D. The contract will be valid only if the buyer was unaware of the mistake.

    E. The contact will not be valid beyond the quantity of the goods.

© COPYRIGHT 2022. Exam SAM Study Aids & Media dba www.examsam.com
This material may not be copied or reproduced in any form.

WORKKEYS WORKPLACE DOCUMENTS PRACTICE TEST 3

Instructions: Read each of the passages below and then answer the questions that follow each one. Select only ONE answer per question. There is no penalty for incorrect answers, so you should guess an answer choice even when you are unsure. You are allowed 55 minutes to answer all 35 questions.

Store Returns Policy (Level 3)

Please note that the store's return policy has changed for the following departments:

<u>Sporting Goods:</u>

Sporting equipment will continue to be accepted for return as per our previous policy.

However, any items of sportwear or other items of clothing sold in the sporting goods department must now be returned within 7 days from the date of purchase.

The only exception to the above policy change is swimwear, which, as before, cannot be returned in any circumstance as per state health and hygiene laws.

<u>Food and Drink:</u>

We now no longer accept fresh fruit or vegetables for returns, unless they were unfit for human consumption on the date of purchase.

As a result of new laws in our country, we now need to ask for identification from anyone returning alcoholic drinks.

Since we now perform damage checks on merchandise at the point of sale, as of today, we will no longer offer refunds for any item that is damaged.

© COPYRIGHT 2022. Exam SAM Study Aids & Media dba www.examsam.com
This material may not be copied or reproduced in any form.

Question 1: Which of the following best describes the main purpose of this document?

    A. To communicate rules for selling sporting goods and food and drink.

    B. To clarify an important change in company policy.

    C. To explain the circumstances in which certain goods can be returned.

    D. To point out exceptions to the company's returns policy.

    E. To remind employees to check goods for damage.

Question 2: A customer wants to return a bikini because she claims that it was torn when she bought it three weeks ago. What should you tell her?

    A. Swimwear cannot be returned because of state laws.

    B. Swimwear must be returned within 7 days of purchase.

    C. She can get a return because swimwear is a sporting good.

    D. The store offers refunds for damaged goods.

    E. You will need to see her identification to process the refund.

© COPYRIGHT 2022. Exam SAM Study Aids & Media dba www.examsam.com
This material may not be copied or reproduced in any form.

MEMO TO ALL STAFF (Level 4)

RE: Changes to the Company's Business Insurance Policy

The following types of damage are now covered and excluded by the Company's business insurance policy.

- **Property Damage:** Physical damage caused by an abrupt and accidental breakdown to the Company's equipment is covered.

- **Business Income & Extra Expense:** Business losses due to temporarily stopping operations because of property being damaged are covered. Necessary expenses incurred to continue operations as a result of a breakdown are also covered.

Exclusions to coverage

Any expense or loss which is not accidental or which is foreseen is excluded from our policy. In other words, damage caused intentionally or by pretermission is not covered.

© COPYRIGHT 2022. Exam SAM Study Aids & Media dba www.examsam.com
This material may not be copied or reproduced in any form.

Question 3: Which of the following situations would be covered by the above policy?

 A. The company loses income because part of the factory is damaged.

 B. The conveyor belt is damaged when an employee intentionally overloads it.

 C. The company has costs associated with machine maintenance.

 D. The company's profits start to decline after the holidays.

 E. The company's copying machine finally breaks down after acting strangely for a few weeks.

Question 4: Which of the following is closest in meaning to the phrase "by pretermission" in the last paragraph of the document?

 A. due to interruption

 B. with deliberation

 C. in advance

 D. with attention

 E. by negligence

© COPYRIGHT 2022. Exam SAM Study Aids & Media dba www.examsam.com
This material may not be copied or reproduced in any form.

VENDING MACHINE REPAIR INSTRUCTIONS FOR TECHNICIANS (Level 4)

If the machine is not vending the product, please check the mechanisms inside the machine in the following order:

1. The first check is the slot. Be sure that it is strait and clear of any debris.

2. The next check is the weighing mechanism, located just in front of the cradle.

3. If the weighing mechanism is sound, then check the magnets along the runway. Test that electricity is passing through the magnets by seeing if coins slow down on the runway. If coins decrease in speed on the runway, the coin is considered real, meaning that the magnets are functioning correctly.

4. Then check the deflector. If the deflector is functional, the coin should fall into the "accept" instead of the "reject" channel.

5. Finally, ensure that the product falls to the receiving bay at the front of the machine.

© COPYRIGHT 2022. Exam SAM Study Aids & Media dba www.examsam.com
This material may not be copied or reproduced in any form.

Question 5: According to the document, if the coin incorrectly falls into the "reject" channel, the technician should first:

    A. clear away any debris.

    B. check the deflector.

    C. test the speed of the coin.

    D. place a coin in the weighing mechanism.

    E. ensure that the product is not vended.

Question 6: Based on the instructions, which mechanisms determine whether the coin is real?

    A. Weighing mechanism and magnets

    B. Magnets and runway

    C. Deflector and accept channel

    D. Accept and reject channels

    E. The slot and receiving bay

© COPYRIGHT 2022. Exam SAM Study Aids & Media dba www.examsam.com
This material may not be copied or reproduced in any form.

Employment Bulletin (Level 5)

Main Points for October 1 to December 31

Estimated annual growth in average weekly earnings for our employees was 1.8% for this quarter. This percentage includes both regular pay (excluding bonuses) and total pay (including bonuses).

All employees saw annual growth in pay of at least 1.7%. This compares favorably with the National Consumer Price Index, which makes adjustments to wages for inflation.

After adjusting for inflation, the annual growth in our regular pay is estimated to be 2.6% and the annual growth in our total pay is estimated to be 3.7%.

The rate of pay growth has trended upwards since May 2017, reaching 3.9% from May to January 2020, the highest nominal "pay growth rate" since 2010. However, pay growth fell back below our targets during the previous quarter. This fallback was the result of a different pattern of pay raises for some employees.

The earnings estimates are not just a measure of pay rises as they also reflect changes in the number of paid hours worked and changes in the structure of the workforce. For example, more highly-paid jobs would have an upward effect on earnings growth rates.

© COPYRIGHT 2022. Exam SAM Study Aids & Media dba www.examsam.com
This material may not be copied or reproduced in any form.

Question 7: In paragraph 4, the word "nominal" most nearly means:

A. of an insignificant amount.

B. assigned to a person by name.

C. falling above the target.

D. being so-named.

E. relating to an upward trend.

Question 8: According to the document, what will happen to the "pay growth rate" if the number of highly-paid jobs suddenly goes up?

A. This may have a disproportionate effect on the pay growth rate percentage.

B. There will be less money available for other jobs.

C. This will make it difficult to estimate the percentage for the following quarter.

D. The earnings estimates will need to be adjusted retroactively.

E. The National Consumer Price Index will need to be taken into account.

© COPYRIGHT 2022. Exam SAM Study Aids & Media dba www.examsam.com
This material may not be copied or reproduced in any form.

Notice to Customers (Level 5)

Average Monthly Billing Calculations

The goal of average monthly billing is to have 12 bills each year that are as close as possible to the same amount. By using average billing, a customer should be able to have a predictable electric bill, similar to their other monthly expenditures like rent or insurance.

We use a formula to determine the amount a customer pays each month.
- Add up the past 12 months' historical kWh readings
- Divide that sum by 12 to get their average monthly electricity usage.
- That average monthly electricity usage is multiplied by a customer's current rate per kWh to determine their average bill.

If a customer hasn't lived in their house for the entire prior 12 months, we will use the historic meter data from the property and the customer's current electricity rate to calculate the average bill.

In the event that a customer wishes to revise their monthly bills, their MkWh must have been steadily declining for at least 6 months.

© COPYRIGHT 2022. Exam SAM Study Aids & Media dba www.examsam.com
This material may not be copied or reproduced in any form.

Question 9: According to the document, average billing is intended to:

A. lower the customer's monthly expenditure for electricity

B. make it easier for the electricity company to issue bills

C. provide expenditure guidelines for customers that move into new homes

D. assist customers who wish to revise their electricity bills

E. help customers better plan for payment of their electricity bills.

Question 10: The acronym MkWh in the last paragraph of the document most likely refers to:

A. the dollar value of the customer's bills each month.

B. the reading on a customer's electricity meter on a given date.

C. the rate of the customer's monthly electricity usage.

D. the dollar value of the customer's bills each year.

E. the past 12 months' historical electricity usage.

© COPYRIGHT 2022. Exam SAM Study Aids & Media dba www.examsam.com
This material may not be copied or reproduced in any form.

Additional Taxes Owing (Level 6)

To: John Jones, Owner, XYZ Company

Tax ID # 12345678

From: State Department of Revenue

Re: Additional Taxes Owing

The Department of Revenue has received information from the Internal Revenue Service suggesting that your company is required to file payroll tax returns.

If you agree with our request for the returns:

Prepare the enclosed return and send it back to us using the pre-addressed envelope provided.

You may engage a tax professional to prepare the return for you.

Please see the Department of Revenue's website if you need to view the instructions for the return.

If you have already filed a payroll tax return and:

The tax ID number provided above is not correct, please return this letter to us with the correct tax ID number.

If the tax ID above is correct, make a copy of the payroll tax return and send it back to us using the pre-addressed envelope provided, together with proof of your payment of the tax or evidence of the refund that your company received.

If you believe that your company is not required to file a payroll tax return:

Send a written explanation to us.

Also send a copy of the income tax return you filed with the IRS, as well as payroll tax returns your company filed in any other state.

Send your explanation and copies of the requested returns back to us using the pre-addressed envelope provided.

© COPYRIGHT 2022. Exam SAM Study Aids & Media dba www.examsam.com
This material may not be copied or reproduced in any form.

Question 11: You work as an auditor for the State Department of Revenue. What is most likely your primary rationale behind sending this document?

    A. to inform the taxpayer about how to file payroll tax returns

    B. to receive payment for any payroll taxes that may be outstanding

    C. to verify the company's tax ID number

    D. to request a copy of the tax return the company filed with the IRS

    E. to remind the taxpayer that a payroll tax return is due

Question 12: Based on the document, what should the company do if it has not already sent in the requested return?

    A. Provide their correct tax ID number

    B. Speak to a tax professional

    C. Send in an explanation and/or the requested returns

    D. Send in the correct tax ID number with the requested returns

    E. Provide a copy of the tax return to the IRS

© COPYRIGHT 2022. Exam SAM Study Aids & Media dba www.examsam.com
This material may not be copied or reproduced in any form.

Instruction Manual for Use of Sealant Machine (Level 6)

Document A

Place the plug for the power supply unit into an electrical socket, paying attention to the voltage indicated on the machine instruction plate. Then connect the sealing wand to the power supply unit by using the special adaptor and plug. Failure to use the appropriate voltage or adaptor will result in irreversible damage to the machine, so particular care should be taken at this point. Next turn the control knob that reads "Sealant Time" on the power supply unit to the left to number "1" while simultaneously depressing Button A. The sealant machine should now be operational and fully functional to use on any materials that conform to those stated in the UIM. Materials should be placed below the sealing wand and closed by lowering the wand onto the materials by manual operation. Before lowering the sealing wand, the operator should ensure that the material is flat and smooth, keeping the material stretched tightly between the sealing beams on either end of the material placement area. As soon as the sealing wand is lowered, the sealant is released and the sealing process will be complete when a loud audible click is heard. Note that when a setting of higher than 1 is used on the control knob, the material should not be removed from the machine for at least 5 seconds after sealing takes place in order for the materials to cool.

Document B

In the event that sealant time needs to be adjusted, then turn the control knob that reads "Sealant Time" to the right while simultaneously depressing button B. The sealing time may only be adjusted in this way, by first setting the control knob counter-clockwise to number 1 and then turning the knob clockwise (while depressing the necessary buttons as indicated in the aforementioned steps in both Documents A and B). Depending upon the types of material to be sealed, as well as the thickness of the material, the operator may wish to attempt a trial sealant on a scrap of material before proceeding. Note that a setting of no higher than 4 is recommended for cellulose film and plastic bags.

© COPYRIGHT 2022. Exam SAM Study Aids & Media dba www.examsam.com
This material may not be copied or reproduced in any form.

Question 13: The acronym UIM in Document A most likely refers to:

    A. a written manual with instructions on how to use the sealant machine

    B. a group of materials of a particular thickness

    C. an organization that governs the use of sealant machines

    D. a storage facility for materials that are to be sealed

    E. a mistake that sometime occurs with sealants

Question 14: According to both documents, what is the last required step in adjusting sealant time?

    A. turning the control knob counter-clockwise while holding button A

    B. turning the control knob clockwise while holding button B

    C. turning the control knob clockwise while holding button A

    D. turning the control knob counter-clockwise while holding button B

    E. depressing button B

© COPYRIGHT 2022. Exam SAM Study Aids & Media dba www.examsam.com
This material may not be copied or reproduced in any form.

Company Obligations to the Customer (Level 6)

Repairs and replacements

If a customer has accepted an item, but later discovers a fault or defect with the item, the Company will repair or replace it. The customer retains the right under law to reject the item after it has been repaired or replaced.

A customer has accepted an item if they have done either of the following:

- told the Company that they have accepted it after having had enough opportunity to inspect the item before confirming that they have received it.

- altered the item.

The company must repair or replace an item if a customer returns it within 6 months, unless the Company can prove it was not faulty when the customer purchased it. The Company has the right to ask a customer to prove an item was faulty when they bought it if the customer asks for a repair or replacement after 6 months from the date of acceptance.

Warranties and guarantees

A customer has the same right to repairs or a replacement regardless of whether they have a warranty or guarantee or not. Therefore, the Company is still under the obligation to repair or replace goods if a customer's warranty or guarantee has run out.

Proof of purchase

The Company has the right to ask the customer for proof that they purchased an item from us. Acceptable forms of proof are digital, electronic, or printed receipts or company invoices or personal or company bank statements indicating the Company as payee.

Items returned by someone other than the buyer

The Company is only under the obligation to accept returns from the person or entity who bought the item from us. Friends, family members, or other third parties wishing to return an item on behalf of the customer must first present permission from the customer in the form of a written statement.

© COPYRIGHT 2022. Exam SAM Study Aids & Media dba www.examsam.com
This material may not be copied or reproduced in any form.

Question 15: According to the document, when is an item considered to be accepted?

    A. when the customer pays for it

    B. when the customer inspects it

    C. if the customer makes modifications to it

    D. when the Company orders it for the customer

    E. if the Company repairs it for the customer

Question 16: What is the Company's obligation for requests for repairs or replacements made less than six months after the purchase of an item?

    A. The Company is under no obligation to repair or replace the item.

    B. The Company must repair the item only if it is covered by a warranty.

    C. The Company must repair or replace the item, but only if the customer has evidence that it was not working when they bought it.

    D. The Company must repair or replace the item, unless it has evidence that it was working when the customer bought it.

    E. The Company must repair or replace the item in any circumstance.

Email to all staff: Please note that electronic communication from a customer to a third party constitutes a written statement for purposes of the last paragraph of our document regarding Company Obligations to the Customer, provided that the email address or phone number of the sender of said communication corresponds to the information on the customer's file.

Question 17: You receive the message above. Based on this message and the document, if a customer calls you to tell you to accept a return for their purchase, which is going to brought back by a friend of the customer, what should you do?

    A. Tell the customer that proof of purchase for the item will need to be provided.

    B. Advise the customer that they need to prove the item is faulty.

    C. Ask whether the customer purchased a guarantee or warrantee.

    D. Check the caller ID on your phone for the customer's phone number.

    E. Advise the customer that they need to send permission for the return via text or email to their friend.

© COPYRIGHT 2022. Exam SAM Study Aids & Media dba www.examsam.com
This material may not be copied or reproduced in any form.

Expense Claim Form Submission (Level 6)

Expenses documents form part of this policy together with the applicable instructions for using such documents. The forms can be downloaded from the "Staff Forms" section of the Company website.

All monthly expense claim forms must be received by the cut-off dates shown on the "Staff Forms" section of the Company website. Extensions to said cut-off dates will not be provided under any circumstances. Any expense claim form received after the monthly cut-off date will be paid to the employee the following month. While the cut-off date is generally the 25th of every month, cut-off dates shall vary when this date falls on a weekend or official national holidays. Incomplete or illegible forms will be returned to the employee, and the normal cut-off time will apply to the corrected expense claim form.

All managerial employees who are authorized to sign expense claims should ensure that the Finance Department holds an up-to-date signatory rights form signed by said managerial employee since the claim cannot be processed if we do not have an up-to-date signatory rights form. Some managers have automatic approval rights for online claim submissions which are less than $100 only, circumventing the need for a signature and signatory rights form in this instance.

It is the responsibility of the authorized signatory to check that the claim details are accurate and correct and to ensure the finance cost codes provided in Column C of the form are correct. Where a managerial employee is required as part of their duties to authorize expense claim forms, they must ensure that all forms are complete and in compliance with these guidelines. Under no circumstances should incomplete or non-compliant forms be approved. The authorized signatory must be senior in staff position to the expense claimant.

Claims should be made at the end of the month for the whole of that month. Where this is not possible due to being away, the claim should be filed the following month. Note that expense claims for expenditures more than three months old will not be paid under any circumstances.

© COPYRIGHT 2022. Exam SAM Study Aids & Media dba www.examsam.com
This material may not be copied or reproduced in any form.

Question 18: What is implied by the phrase "automatic approval rights" in paragraph 3 of the document?
   A. The expense claim forms of managers are automatically approved.
   B. Expense claims less than $100 do not need to be approved.
   C. Expense claims less than $100 do not need to be checked.
   D. Managers don't need to sign online claims under $100.
   E. The Finance Department doesn't need the appropriate manager to file a signatory rights form.

Question 19: According to the document, which of the following procedures is not applicable when incomplete or illegible expense claims are received?
   A. The corrected form will need to be re-signed.
   B. The Finance Department will need to have a current signatory rights form.
   C. The person signing the corrected form needs to check the cost codes provided.
   D. The staff member signing the form needs to be senior to the employee claiming the expense.
   E. The employee will be granted more time to make the corrections.

Question 20: According to the document, what should you do if you receive an expense claim form for a $90 expenditure that was made by the employee four months ago?
   A. Process the claim since it is less than $100.
   B. Ask the employee if they have been away.
   C. Deny the claim because it has been filed too late.
   D. Approve the claim if it was made online.
   E. Check the appropriate signatory rights form.

© COPYRIGHT 2022. Exam SAM Study Aids & Media dba www.examsam.com
This material may not be copied or reproduced in any form.

Company Pension Plan Policy (Level 7)

1.1 All employees have non-discriminatory access to the 401(k) plan [hereinafter referred to as the 401(k) or the plan] established by the Company. Specifically, Company policy prohibits exclusions from plan participation that are based on personal criteria such as age, gender identification, sexual preference, marital status, religion, nationality, or length of service. The Company policy also prohibits exclusions from plan participation based on salary level, or whether an employee is classified as being employed on a full-time, part-time, short-term, or long-term basis. State and Federal regulation of 401(k) plans similarly guarantees broad access to such plans, although the extent of such access may take into account factors such as the unique needs of the employer establishing the plan. The Company acknowledges that the 401(k) will serve as the primary means of providing retirement income for many employees, and employees that are excluded from participation in the plan, as well as those that participate in the plan, may wish to seek independent financial advice for their retirement planning.

1.2 Employees shall be equally treated under the plan with respect to governance, portability rights, disclosure requirements, redress mechanisms, and any other rights associated with the plan.

1.3 When establishing rules for benefit levels and accrual or contribution rates, the Company shall take the extent of public sources of retirement income such as Social Security Retirement Benefit into account in order to determine the adequacy of the totality of the retirement income employees may receive.

1.4 Employees are absolutely protected from retaliatory actions and threats of retaliation by their employer or 401(k) plan representatives when filing a complaint about the plan under their rights of plan participation. For instance, employees are protected from terminations of employment to be carried out with the intent to prevent the vesting of an accrued benefit under the plan. Similarly, individuals exercising their rights to file an appeal to the outcome of their complaint or employees undertaking administrative or judicial action against the Company or the plan are protected from retaliatory action, such as termination of employment, suspension of portability upon termination, suspension of employment, discipline, or fines.

© COPYRIGHT 2022. Exam SAM Study Aids & Media dba www.examsam.com
This material may not be copied or reproduced in any form.

Question 21: According to the document, which of the following constitutes a valid reason to exclude someone from the 401(k) plan?

A. The person works for the company on a casual, as-needed basis.

B. The person hasn't worked for the company long enough.

C. The person is eligible for large monthly retirement benefits from social security.

D. The person is not a citizen of the United States.

E. The person refused to seek independent financial advice about retirement.

Question 22: According to the document, what factors may affect the Company's contribution rate to the plan?

A. The number of terminations they have had to make in previous years.

B. Factors that apply exclusively to the Company, like its historical financial performance.

C. The value of collective benefits already accruing in the plan.

D. The number of employees that are to become vested in the plan.

E. Whether a judicial action is outstanding against the Company's plan.

Question 23: What is most likely meant by the phrase "portability rights" in section 1.2 of the document?

A. An employee can move the money from the plan to new employer's plan.

B. Employees remain entitled to benefits if they are promoted.

C. Employee benefits will be moved if they are transferred to an office of the Company in a different city.

D. Employees will retain their benefits when receiving a promotion.

E. Employees can withdraw their money from the plan at any time.

© COPYRIGHT 2022. Exam SAM Study Aids & Media dba www.examsam.com
This material may not be copied or reproduced in any form.

MERGER AGREEMENT (Level 7)

From and after the merger date, the present bylaws of ABC, the company being acquired, shall be and become the bylaws of the surviving corporation until they shall be altered, amended or repealed, or until new bylaws shall be adopted, in accordance with the provisions of law, the bylaws, and the certificate of incorporation of the surviving corporation.

On the merger date, all property, real, personal and mixed, and all debts due to ABC on whatever account, as well for stock subscriptions as all other choses in action, and all and every other interest of or belonging to ABC shall be taken by and deemed to be transferred to and vested in the surviving corporation without further act or deed; and all property and every other interest shall be as effectually the property of the surviving corporation as it was of ABC, and the title to any real estate or any interest, whether vested by deed or otherwise, shall not revert or be in any way impaired by reason of the merger; and all rights of creditors and all liens upon the property of ABC shall be preserved unimpaired, and all these rights and debts, liabilities, obligations, and duties of ABC shall attach to the surviving corporation, and may be enforced against it to the same extent as if the debts, liabilities, obligations, and duties had been incurred or contracted by it.

Any action or proceeding either pending by or against ABC may be prosecuted to judgment as if the merger had not taken place. The parties respectively agree that from time to time, when requested by the surviving corporation or by its successors or assigns, they will execute and deliver or cause to be executed and delivered all deeds and instruments, and will take or cause to be taken all further or other action, as the surviving corporation may deem necessary or desirable in order to vest in and confirm to the surviving corporation or its successors or assigns title to and possession of all the property and rights and otherwise carry out the intent and purposes of this agreement.

© COPYRIGHT 2022. Exam SAM Study Aids & Media dba www.examsam.com
This material may not be copied or reproduced in any form.

Question 24: According to the document, which one of the following does ABC need to do before the date of the merger?

A. Pay off any outstanding debts that it currently owes.

B. Deliver any documents to the surviving corporation if they request them.

C. Transfer any stock subscriptions to the surviving corporation.

D. Vest any interests in deeds in the surviving corporation.

E. Ensure that the rights of creditors in any liens remain unimpaired.

Question 25: According to the document, what will happen if another company has a lawsuit against ABC on the date of the merger?

A. ABC will remain liable for any action under the lawsuit.

B. The surviving corporation will take the place of ABC in the lawsuit.

C. ABC and the surviving corporation will be jointly liable.

D. ABC will remain liable for actions in the lawsuit relating only to real estate.

E. The liability for such a lawsuit would need to be determined by the court.

Question 26: Before the merger agreement is signed, ABC corporation owns a 100,000 square foot warehouse that has a loan against it. What will happen to this loan after the merger is signed?

A. The payments on the loan will remain the responsibility of ABC if their right to the loan is unimpaired.

B. The payments on the loan will remain the responsibility of ABC if their right to the loan is vested by deed or otherwise.

C. The payments on it will be taken on by the surviving corporation like the rest of ABC's debts.

D. The payments on it will be taken on by the surviving corporation, only if there is a lien on the property.

E. The payments on it will be taken on by the surviving corporation only if their rights are unimpaired.

© COPYRIGHT 2022. Exam SAM Study Aids & Media dba www.examsam.com
This material may not be copied or reproduced in any form.

Bulletin RE: Returning Residents (Level 7)

This bulletin provides interested parties with information about who is considered a returning resident under the Country's Immigration Rules. When a person holds permission to enter or remain in the Country and they leave the Country for any reason, on their return, their residency status shall be determined based on the requirements stated in the following rules. The person's new status will depend on the amount of time spent outside the Country.

Less than 2 years' absence

A person who has been absent from the Country for less than 2 years will retain their permission to remain in the Country and will not need to apply for entry clearance before returning to their residence in the Country. Border force control officers will assess whether a person may be admitted for entry to the Country under the requirements of the Passport Office.

2 years' or more absence

A person who has been absent from the Country for more than 2 consecutive years will automatically lose their permission to remain in the Country as a matter of law. The exception to this is only for residents who took up residence in the Country prior to January 1, 1975. Such residents are protected from losing permission to remain in the Country due to absences outside the Country until December 31, 2035, when this grandfather clause shall be revoked. After this date, any permission to remain in the Country will be lost following an absence of 2 years or more.

There are some further exceptions which prevent a person's permission to remain in the Country from lapsing. Further provisions have been made to ensure that any period spent outside the Country will not count towards the calculation of the 2-year period for the following people: a spouse or child who accompanies a member of the Armed Forces overseas; a spouse or child accompanying someone classified as a High-Level Diplomat for the Country; or those who have been employed overseas as foreign employees of the country.

A person who has been absent for more than 2 years must apply for entry clearance as a returning resident and will be assessed by Entry Clearance Officers.

© COPYRIGHT 2022. Exam SAM Study Aids & Media dba www.examsam.com
This material may not be copied or reproduced in any form.

Question 27: According to the document, what happens when a resident's absence from the Country is under two years?

    A. Their passport will not need to be checked upon entry to the Country.

    B. They may return as resident, but will require special clearance.

    C. They may return if their status was obtained prior to January 1, 1975.

    D. They may return, provided that they meet one of the requirements in the final paragraph of the document.

    E. They will not have to reapply for permission to remain in the Country.

Question 28: According to the document, what does the phrase "grandfather clause" in paragraph 3 refer to?

    A. The fact that certain people may automatically lose their residence.

    B. The statement that permission to remain in the Country is "a matter of law."

    C. The provision that certain periods of time will not count towards any given two-year period.

    D. The exception provided for residence obtained before January 1, 1975.

    E. The exclusion for those who enter as residents before December 31, 2035.

Question 29: Which one of the following best describes the rationale behind the fourth paragraph of the document?

    A. To allow more generous residency rules for families providing service to the Country in some way.

    B. To protect the needs of marital partners and children.

    C. To encourage more people to go into work for the Country overseas.

    D. To show gratitude to those having served in the Armed Forces of the Country.

    E. To protect the families of foreign employees and high-level diplomats.

© COPYRIGHT 2022. Exam SAM Study Aids & Media dba www.examsam.com
This material may not be copied or reproduced in any form.

7 U.S. Code § 281 & 284 – Honeybee importation & Eradication and control of undesirable species and subspecies (Level 7)

§ 281 (a) IN GENERAL
The Secretary of Agriculture is authorized to prohibit or restrict the importation or entry of honeybees into or through the United States in order to prevent the introduction and spread of diseases and parasites harmful to honeybees, the introduction of genetically undesirable germ plasm of honeybees, or the introduction and spread of undesirable species or subspecies of honeybees.

(b) REGULATIONS
The Secretary of Agriculture and the Secretary of the Treasury are each authorized to prescribe such regulations as the respective Secretary determines necessary to carry out this section.

(c) ENFORCEMENT
Honeybees offered for importation into, intercepted entering, or having entered the United States, other than in accordance with regulations promulgated by the Secretary of Agriculture and the Secretary of the Treasury, shall be destroyed or immediately exported.

(d) "HONEYBEE" DEFINED
As used in this chapter, the term "honeybee" means all life stages and the germ plasm of honeybees of the genus Apis, excepting honey from said bees.

§ 284 (a) OPERATIONS IN UNITED STATES
The Secretary of Agriculture either independently or in cooperation with States or political subdivisions thereof, farmers' associations, and similar organizations and individuals, is authorized to carry out operations or measures in the United States to eradicate, suppress, control, and to prevent or retard the spread of undesirable species and subspecies of honeybees.

(b) COOPERATION WITH CERTAIN FOREIGN GOVERNMENTS; MEASURE AND CHARACTER; CONSULTATION WITH SECRETARY OF STATE
The Secretary of Agriculture is authorized to cooperate with the Governments of Canada, Mexico, Guatemala, Belize, Honduras, El Salvador, Nicaragua, Costa Rica, Panama, and Colombia, or the local authorities thereof, in carrying out necessary research, surveys, and control operations in those countries in connection with the eradication, suppression, control, and prevention or retardation of the spread of undesirable pathogens, including but not limited to those from Apis mellifera adansonii. The measure and character of cooperation

© COPYRIGHT 2022. Exam SAM Study Aids & Media dba www.examsam.com
This material may not be copied or reproduced in any form.

carried out under this subsection on the part of such countries, including the expenditure or use of funds appropriated pursuant to this chapter, shall be such as may be prescribed by the Secretary of Agriculture. Arrangements for the cooperation authorized by this subsection shall be made through and in consultation with the Secretary of State.

Question 30: What is the most likely explanation of the phrase "Apis mellifera adansonii" in Section 284(b) of the document?
   A. It is the name of an importation treaty signed by one of the countries mentioned previously in this section.
   B. It refers to a region in one of the countries mentioned previously in this section.
   C. It is a particular species or subspecies of honeybees.
   D. It is a certain proclamation signed by the Secretary of Agriculture.
   E. It is a kind of honey from a certain species of honeybees.

Question 31: According to the document, how is the Secretary of the Treasury involved in governing the importation of honeybees?
   A. It works closely with the Secretary of State when needed.
   B. It establishes rules and regulations for these types of importations.
   C. It works to intercept illegal deliveries of honeybees.
   D. It immediately exports or destroys illegal importations of honeybees.
   E. It investigates the control and eradication of undesirable species of bees.

Question 32: You work for the Secretary of Agriculture. You have been informed that a shipment of Columbian honeybees is about to arrive in the United States. What action should you take?
   A. Check whether the shipment contains any germ plasm from the honeybees.
   B. Take action to intercept the delivery.
   C. Destroy the bees immediately.
   D. Check whether the importation conforms to the promulgated regulations.
   E. Allow the importation since Columbia works in cooperation with the Secretary of State.

© COPYRIGHT 2022. Exam SAM Study Aids & Media dba www.examsam.com
This material may not be copied or reproduced in any form.

AGREEMENT FOR THE PROVISION OF INTRODUCTIONS TO NEW BUSINESS (Level 7)

Collectively known as the **Parties,** or individually as a **Party.**
IT IS AGREED as follows:

1. Introductions, Introductory Commission

1.1. The Introducer may from time to time make Introductions for the purpose of developing business for the Client, and the Introduced Client agrees and undertakes to reward the Introducer for such Introductions in accordance with clauses 1.2, 1.3, and 1.4.

1.2. If, following the making of an Introduction, an Introduced Client engages the Client within 12 months of the introduction, for the provision of its services, the Introduced Client must pay to the Introducer the Introductory Commission in respect of each such Introduction.

1.3. The Introductory Commission is a sum equal to 5% of the amount of the first year's fees invoiced directly or indirectly by the Engaged Party for the provision of its services.

1.4. The Introductory Commission shall become payable on the final date of each month, at which time the Engaged Party shall raise an invoice in respect of the work undertaken by it in respect of the Introduction or Relevant Transaction.

1.5. Both Parties shall ensure that all invoices raised in respect of any fees on which a commission payment is due under this Agreement are to be raised promptly on the last day of each month and a copy of each such invoice shall be provided to the other Party within 7 days of being raised.

1.6. Payment of the Introductory Commission shall be made by the Introduced Client within 14 days of the other Party raising its invoice in this regard.

2. Late or non-payment

2.1. If the Introduced Client fails to pay any amount payable by it under this Agreement, the Introducer shall be entitled to charge the Introduced Client interest on the overdue amount, from the due date up to the date of actual payment, after as well as before judgment, at the rate of 10% per annum. Such interest shall accrue on a daily basis and be compounded monthly.

2.2 The Introducer may file any unpaid invoice as a non-payment dispute with the appropriate jurisdiction.

© COPYRIGHT 2022. Exam SAM Study Aids & Media dba www.examsam.com
This material may not be copied or reproduced in any form.

3. Further Covenants

3.1 The Client must conduct her/himself in a proper, skillful, and professional manner in accordance with the Introduced Organization's Code of Professional Conduct.

3.2 The Client shall not agree to any further work with a client that is a competitor to the Introduced Client for similar or related work without first receiving the agreement of the Introducer, and shall not solicit further work from a competitor client directly for similar or related work.

Question 33: Which one of the following is the best explanation of the phrase "Introduced Client' as it is used in the document?

 A. A party who hires someone after meeting that person via the Introducer

 B. A party who is introduced to potential clients by the Introducer.

 C. A party who may be required to pay an Introductory Commission

 D. A party who is a competitor of an "Engaged Party"

 E. This phrase is synonymous with "Engaged Party"

Question 34: According to the document, what would be the maximum number of days from the date of introduction that an Introducer would need to wait for Payment, without late fees being incurred?

 A. A year plus one month and 7 days

 B. A year plus one month and 14 days

 C. A year plus one month and 21 days

 D. One month and 14 days

 E. One month and 21 days

Question 35: You are an Introducer. You discover that an Introduced Client engaged one of your clients fourteen months ago without informing you. The Introduced Client claims that they do not intend to pay you any introductory commission. What action should you take first?

 A. Determine the amount of fees paid by the Introduced Party to the Engaged Party during its first 12 months of service.

 B. Determine the amount of fees paid by the Engaged Party to the Client during the first 12 months of service.

 C. Investigate whether any competitor was also engaged by the Introduced Client.

 D. Prepare an invoice for the Client with accrued interest.

 E. File a legal judgment for non-payment against the Introduced Client.

© COPYRIGHT 2022. Exam SAM Study Aids & Media dba www.examsam.com
This material may not be copied or reproduced in any form.

Answer Key – Practice Test 1

1. B

2. E

3. C

4. D

5. A

6. D

7. A

8. B

9. E

10. B

11. C

12. A

13. C

14. E

15. C

16. D

17. A

18. E

19. B

© COPYRIGHT 2022. Exam SAM Study Aids & Media dba www.examsam.com
This material may not be copied or reproduced in any form.

20. A

21. E

22. D

23. C

24. A

25. B

26. D

27. A

28. E

29. E

30. C

31. D

32. E

33. A

34. B

35. E

© COPYRIGHT 2022. Exam SAM Study Aids & Media dba www.examsam.com
This material may not be copied or reproduced in any form.

Answer Key – Practice Test 2

1. C

2. B

3. A

4. C

5. E

6. D

7. C

8. D

9. E

10. B

11. D

12. E

13. D

14. B

15. A

16. E

17. B

18. A

19. D

© COPYRIGHT 2022. Exam SAM Study Aids & Media dba www.examsam.com
This material may not be copied or reproduced in any form.

20. D

21. D

22. E

23. B

24. A

25. B

26. A

27. C

28. C

29. D

30. A

31. D

32. E

33. B

34. C

35. A

© COPYRIGHT 2022. Exam SAM Study Aids & Media dba www.examsam.com
This material may not be copied or reproduced in any form.

Answer Key – Practice Test 3

1. C

2. A

3. A

4. E

5. B

6. B

7. D

8. A

9. E

10. C

11. B

12. C

13. A

14. B

15. C

16. D

17. E

18. D

19. E

© COPYRIGHT 2022. Exam SAM Study Aids & Media dba www.examsam.com
This material may not be copied or reproduced in any form.

20. C

21. A

22. B

23. A

24. B

25. A

26. C

27. E

28. D

29. A

30. C

31. B

32. D

33. A

34. C

35. A

© COPYRIGHT 2022. Exam SAM Study Aids & Media dba www.examsam.com
This material may not be copied or reproduced in any form.

Answers and Explanations – Practice Test 1

1. The correct answer is B. The main purpose of the document is stated in the first sentence: "Employees must be well-groomed and well-dressed." Answer choice A is incorrect because a mission statement of a company sets out in broad terms the aims, goals, and policies of a company. Answer choices C, D, and E are specific points from the document, rather than the general, main purpose.

2. The correct answer is E. Support for the other answer choices can be found in the last paragraph of the document. Filing a form is not mentioned anywhere in the document.

3. The correct answer is C. You work in the restaurant, so you are dealing with the guest discount for meals. Therefore, you need the information from fourth point of the first bulleted list, which states: "Write your signature and the date on the 10% Guest Discount for Meals Ticket." Note that the ticket has already been labeled "Guest Discount for Meals."

4. The correct answer is D. Non-member guests are allowed permission to enter the spa only if they come with a member. The member must present their own card; the guests cannot do this by themselves. The first two points of the second part of the document state: "The member must accompany his or her guest for the spa treatment. If the member does not show their Elite Status Card, please ask them to do so."

© COPYRIGHT 2022. Exam SAM Study Aids & Media dba www.examsam.com
This material may not be copied or reproduced in any form.

5.   The correct answer is A. For questions like this one, pay special attention to where the acronym is placed. The acronym CHA-4 is placed just before the phrase "international orders." The acronym therefore functions as an adjective, which describes the international orders.

6.   The correct answer is D. The last paragraph of the text states: "If the packages are not sorted correctly, they will not be able to be weighed and will be rejected for shipping. In this case, the shipments of the customer's order will be delayed more than five days." All damaged packages must go in container E, regardless of the weight of the package. So, a 32-ounce damaged package has to go in container E, not container B.

7.   The correct answer is A. Paragraph 1 explains that all "completed forms should be submitted to the Vice President of Human Resources."

8.   The correct answer is B. Paragraph 2 states that "what happened, how it happened, and any other factors leading to the event must also be included. Be as specific as possible and attach additional sheets if needed for the description." So, the phrase "attach additional sheets if needed" refers to further details about "other factors leading to the event." Note that a description of the injury is to be included on Part A of the form, rather than on additional sheets.

9.   The correct answer is E. If a customer cancels a reservation 72 hours in advance, or indeed at any time, they will lose their $10 deposit. The

© COPYRIGHT 2022. Exam SAM Study Aids & Media dba www.examsam.com
This material may not be copied or reproduced in any form.

"Deposits" section of the document clarifies that "Guests are required to pay a $10 deposit per room per night in order to make a reservation. Our agreement to accommodate a guest is a legal contract and any deposit paid by the guest to reserve a room is not refundable under any circumstances."

10. The correct answer is B. The last paragraph of the cancellation section states: "If a guest cancels less than 48 hours in advance of the proposed stay and we do not succeed in re-booking the room, the guest will not be liable for the full balance, but there will be a 30% cancellation fee and a 10% administration fee." So, in that case, the guest would lose the deposit in addition to 40% of the price of the room. If the guest cancels more than 48 hours in advance or if the room is later filled, the guest will only lose the $10 deposit.

11. The correct answer is C. The acronym C1 refers to a person who receives goods who is not the original owner. The "Consignee Name" section of the document states that "CN is the name of the original owner of the goods or the equipment. C1 indicates that the goods will be shipped to a different party."

12. The correct answer is A. The two codes PU and HM may not be required in certain situations. The acronym PU refers to the Pickup Party. The document points out that "the PU is only required for pick-ups by road if the

© COPYRIGHT 2022. Exam SAM Study Aids & Media dba www.examsam.com
This material may not be copied or reproduced in any form.

PU differs from the SN." The acronym HM refers to Hazmat Information, and this code should be used "only if a hazardous commodity is being shipped."

13. The correct answer is C. If the machine starts to run unusually fast or if any other fault occurs, you should report it to a superior immediately. The final paragraph entitled "Safety Compliance" explains: "In the event that any usual activity should appear with any of the mechanisms of or in any of the procedures mentioned above, the employee should inform a member of the senior management team immediately."

14. The correct answer is E. The primary rationale behind the document is to clarify the procedures applicable to operating and storing the conveyor belt. While we do not know whether electric shocks have been on the rise recently, the other answer options are specific points, rather than the general rationale.

15. The correct answer is C. The reader can surmise that instructions for certain new schedules have not been provided. The document provides specific instructions on schedules 1 to 4. However, paragraph 1 states that the new tax return "has ten new numbered schedules, in addition to the existing alphabetical schedules." So, instructions are not provided in the document for six of the numbered schedules and all of the alphabetical schedules.

16. The correct answer is D. The final paragraph states: "Please see the RTCB for further information on claiming tax credits." It is sometimes helpful on

© COPYRIGHT 2022. Exam SAM Study Aids & Media dba www.examsam.com
This material may not be copied or reproduced in any form.

acronym questions to see whether the acronym possibly refers to any phrase mentioned in the same paragraph. The paragraph is talking about the refundable tax credit (RTC), so we can infer that the RTCB is something that relates to the RTC. So, the acronym RTCB most likely refers to a separate instructional booklet that explains the refundable tax credit.

17. The correct answer is A. The client has a salary, a property sale, and a tax credit relating to self-employment. So, the tax return should include schedule 1 to report the salary and the property sale, schedule 2 for the self-employment activity (which they will have if taking a self-employment tax credit), schedule 3 for the tax on the property sale (because they will need to calculate the tax due on the property sale or show a calculation that no tax is due), and schedule 4 for the credit on the self-employment activity. The four schedules need to be attached to form UTF, as explained in the first paragraph of the document.

18. The correct answer is E. Before proceeding, you should ensure that the rides pose no risk to public health or safety. The last paragraph states: "waivers may be granted in the event that any such requirements are found not to be necessary in the pervasive interest of public health or safety." The word "pervasive" implies that health and safety affect everything else. If there is a risk, there would be no need to consider anything else, including zoning, amendments, or site usage. So, the most efficient course of action

© COPYRIGHT 2022. Exam SAM Study Aids & Media dba www.examsam.com
This material may not be copied or reproduced in any form.

would be to assess the risk before considering anything else. You may be tempted to choose answer A, but checking zoning ordinances is part of the approval process, and the question is asking about what to do before the approval process.

19. The correct answer is B. A building permit should be obtained once the site plan has been approved. Section 2(b) states: "When the City Council grants an authorization to approve a Site Plan pursuant to this section, the terms thereof shall condition the issuance and collection of a building permit upon said approval." So, when the Site Plan is approved, a building permit needs to be obtained.

20. The correct answer is A. The Site Plan would not be disapproved because it lacks a provision for parking facilities. Answer B is incorrect because, according to Section 1, a plan can only cover "a single parcel of land," not two parcels. Answer C is incorrect because Section 2(a) states that the use of the land must be legally permitted. Answer D is incorrect because Section 2(b) explains that a building permit must be obtained. Answer E is incorrect since Section 3 points out that restrictions or limits may be placed on certain proposals.

21. The correct answer is E. If the cloud in which the Work Management System (WMS) is based were to be compromised, then there would be problems with the functioning of the WMS. We can conclude this because

© COPYRIGHT 2022. Exam SAM Study Aids & Media dba www.examsam.com
This material may not be copied or reproduced in any form.

the first sentence of the document states: "Our new Work Management System (WMS) provides our Company with a cloud-based, warehouse management system." The final paragraph states that the system is "integrated with updates," so answer A is incorrect. Paragraph 1 states that warehousers can be added, so answer B is incorrect. Paragraph 3 describes how the number of orders can be increased, so answer C is incorrect. Paragraph 2 mentions that PDA devices can be connected to the system, so answer D is incorrect.

22. The correct answer is D. The 3PL providers mentioned in paragraph 1 are most likely storage or delivery providers. Remember to look for synonyms in the same paragraph in which the acronym is provided. Paragraph 1 describes pick-pack-delivery providers (who provide deliveries), as well as warehousers (who provide storage).

23. The correct answer is C. The word "scalable" means that a system or operation is designed so that it can grow and expand with ease. Paragraph 3 describes how the number of orders covered by the system can be easily changed. You may be tempted to choose answer A, but this refers to the speed of the system, not the scalability.

24. The correct answer is A. If a shipment arrives at the port, but then leaves without returning, then no payment is owing. This is covered by US Code Section 1315(b), which is provided in the last paragraph. The pertinent

© COPYRIGHT 2022. Exam SAM Study Aids & Media dba www.examsam.com
This material may not be copied or reproduced in any form.

words from that paragraph are as follows: "Any article which has been entered for consumption but which [. . .] is removed from the port [. . .] shall be subject to duty [. . .] but only if the article is returned to such port or place within ninety days after the date of removal [. . .]"

25. The correct answer is B. Section 1552 is most likely used to describe a certain category of goods. Section (a)(2) refers "to an entry for immediate transportation made at the port of original importation under section 1552." The entire document is talking about the movement of goods by entry into port, so we can assume that Section 1552 refers to a type of goods.

26. The correct answer is D. An article that is in port but that has not been sent by mail and that is not subject to sections 1490, 1505, or 1552 is subject to a custom rate that was in effect when the paperwork for the shipment was filed. The applicable words from the first paragraph of the document are as follows: "Except as otherwise specially provided for [in sections 1490, 1505, or 1552], the rate or rates of duty imposed [. . .] on any article [. . .] shall be the rate or rates in effect when the documents comprising the entry [. . .] have been deposited with the Customs Service."

27. The correct answer is A. If you have received indisputable proof that an associate who was terminated 18 months ago is now sharing trade secrets with a competitor, you should terminate the associate's transition payments immediately. Section D of the document explains that "Associate's commission of any other act that is materially harmful to the Company's

© COPYRIGHT 2022. Exam SAM Study Aids & Media dba www.examsam.com
This material may not be copied or reproduced in any form.

business interests during the Transition Period, will, at a minimum, result in the immediate termination of the Transition Payments." We know from paragraph 1, that the transition period covers the two years after an employee's termination of employment. We can surmise that sharing trade secrets with a competitor would be materially harmful to the company. So, the transitions payments should be terminated immediately.

28. The correct answer is E. An associate who quits without giving any notice is not eligible for transition payments, according to the document. Section B of the document states: "No Transition Payments will be paid if Associate voluntarily resigns or retires from employment with the Company."

29. The correct answer is E. The final paragraph pertains to other plans or programs. This paragraph states that the Associate's right to participate in these plans and programs is "non-transferrable," meaning that the right cannot be passed on to any other person. All of the other conditions in the agreement relate only to the Transitions Payments.

30. The correct answer is C. The primary purpose of the rules is to clarify how vacation days are to be used and accrued. Section 1 describes who can accrue vacation days. Sections 2.1 to 2.3 talk about how vacation days can be used. Section 2.4 describes how vacation days are accrued. The remainder of the document provides some specific exceptions to this.

© COPYRIGHT 2022. Exam SAM Study Aids & Media dba www.examsam.com
This material may not be copied or reproduced in any form.

31. The correct answer is D. A part-time employee who has worked for the company for 7 years is entitled to 120 maximum accrued vacation hours, not 260 accrued vacation hours. Section 2.4 states: "The maximum number of vacation hours permitted to be accumulated is 120 hours (15 days) during the first 5 continuous years of employment and thereafter." This limit is only lifted after the "employee's 10-year anniversary of continuous employment." Note that according to section 2.4.1, both part-time and full-time employees are eligible for vacation pay.

32. The correct answer is E. If an employee wants to reschedule her entire vacation, her request needs to be decided upon by a boss of the HR Manager. This specific situation is not described by the document, and the last paragraph states: "Any vacation day requests that fall outside of the situations enumerated in this policy shall be referred to a superior in the HR Department, pending his or her discretionary decision on the matter."

33. The correct answer is A. Section 1.ii of the document states: "Other organized educational and technical programs [. . .] which have been pre-approved by the State prior to the Accountant participating in the program" may be included. You know that her other courses were at a university, so they are eligible under section 1.i. However, you don't know whether her other courses have been pre-approved. So, you would need to ask whether her online courses were approved by the State in advance of her taking them.

© COPYRIGHT 2022. Exam SAM Study Aids & Media dba www.examsam.com
This material may not be copied or reproduced in any form.

34. The correct answer is B. Credits that aren't offered by an accredited university or that have not been approved by the State are not acceptable and should be disallowed, based on the rules stated in sections 1.i and 1.ii. The accountant should be informed of this as soon as possible so that he can rectify the shortcoming during the grace period. Note that the document makes no mention of retroactive approval for courses after they have been taken.

35. The correct answer is E. We know that 120 hours of credit needs to be earned during a three-year period, but the document does not state that an equal number of hours need to be earned each year. For example, an accountant could do all of their educational requirements within the first year, and no educational activities in years 2 and 3 of the three-year period, as long as they achieved 120-hours worth of credit in total. So, we cannot make any assessment about how many hours would be acceptable per each year of the three-year period.

© COPYRIGHT 2022. Exam SAM Study Aids & Media dba www.examsam.com
This material may not be copied or reproduced in any form.

Answers and Explanations – Practice Test 2

1.   The correct answer is C. The primary purpose of the document is to inform Jonas to treat staff on the software update team to a meal out. We know from the first paragraph of the document that Jonas was responsible for the software update. Paragraph 2 then states: "Next week, please plan a day to take yourself and your staff to lunch at the Ivy Restaurant. The meal will on the company account, to thank everyone for all of their hard work."

2.   The correct answer is B. After the meal has taken place, Jonas should provide proof of the expense from the restaurant to a representative in HR. The last paragraph of the letter explains that Jonas should "submit the receipt for the meal to Fatima in HR."

3.   The correct answer is A. If a customer did not see merchandise before purchasing it, you should grant a refund for the item if they do not wish to keep it. The third item of the first section explains that "you do not have to refund a customer if they no longer want an item (unless they bought it without seeing it)." In other words, if a customer bought an item without seeing it, you have to offer a refund if they no longer want it.

4.   The correct answer is C. If a customer wants to return an item that is out of its original box, you should determine whether the item has a flaw or fault. According to the last point of the second section of the document: "You

© COPYRIGHT 2022. Exam SAM Study Aids & Media dba www.examsam.com
This material may not be copied or reproduced in any form.

must offer a refund for the following items, but only if they are defective: any other item that is unboxed or unwrapped." So, first you must determine if the item is defective.

5.   The correct answer is E. If you need an employee ID card after January 1, you will not necessarily need to log on to the company's website. According to the first paragraph of the document, you would only need to log on to the company's website to check your status, but doing so is not compulsory.

6.   The correct answer is D. It is true that the employee ID number on employee ID cards issued before January 1 had 12 numbers. The last paragraph points out that "any cards issued prior to January 1 will have 12-digit ID numbers."

7.   The correct answer is C. The word "charitable" is the closest to the meaning of the word "eleemosynary" as it is used in the document. Remember that for word-meaning questions like this one, you should look for synonyms for the unknown word in the same paragraph as the unknown word. In the next sentence of the document, we can see that the word "charity" is used to describe the organization, so the activities of the organization are charitable.

8.   The correct answer is D. If you are the financial manager for the company, your most important activity for June would be to drive more sales to the store via the fundraising drive. While you may be concerned with the goals mentioned in the other answer choices, as financial manager, your primary

© COPYRIGHT 2022. Exam SAM Study Aids & Media dba www.examsam.com
This material may not be copied or reproduced in any form.

interest would be your own company's financial goals. We can see this in the last sentence of the document, which states: "we sincerely hope that you will visit us this June to take the opportunity to contribute to a good cause, as well as take home some new clothes."

9. The correct answer is E. According to document, in order to apply for the MFLS, an applicant needs to own more than ten acres of the appropriate kind of land. The final sentence of the first paragraph explains that "any owner of more than 10 continuous acres of non-commercial forest land in any town or city may apply for the subsidy."

10. The correct answer is B. If the applicant is operating a hotel on part of the land, you would need to advise them that the subsidy is for non-business land owners only. The first paragraph of the document points out that the subsidy is for "individual [i.e., non-business] property owners."

11. The correct answer is D. You should tell the client that the $45 additional charge consists of a $35 late fee and $10 interest. Payment of this invoice is one month overdue. The first paragraph of the "Payment for Services Rendered" section states: "Should the Client fail to pay the Provider the full amount specified in any invoice within 7 calendar days of the invoice's date, a late fee equal to $35 shall be added to the amount due and interest of 12 percent per annum shall accrue from the calendar day following the invoice's date." An interest rate of 12% per annum equates to an

© COPYRIGHT 2022. Exam SAM Study Aids & Media dba www.examsam.com
This material may not be copied or reproduced in any form.

approximate monthly rate of 1%, and 1% of the $1,000 balance of the invoice equals $10 of interest.

12. The correct answer is E. The "Payment for Services Rendered" Section discusses the terms of payment and outlines the late fees and interest due. You may be tempted to choose answer A, since the last paragraph states: "Neither party shall be liable to perform their obligations under this contract where such failure or delay is beyond the reasonable control of the parties." However, remaining in business would be considered to be within the control of the Client.

13. The correct answer is D. Because the contractor's personal details are publicly available, you should apologize to him for the error and try to get the invoice taken down. Although the worker is an independent contractor, rather than an employee, he would qualify as any "other interested party" as defined in paragraph 1 of the document. Paragraph 4 of the "Policy Elements" section explains that "data will not be [. . .] distributed to any third party," and publication via the internet violates this policy, so an apology should be given and the mistake should be rectified.

14. The correct answer is B. From the "Actions" section of the document, we can infer that the company regards their data protection procedures as something that can be constantly improved. The last paragraph states: "In order to improve our data protection procedures, we're committed to monitoring access to data . . ."

© COPYRIGHT 2022. Exam SAM Study Aids & Media dba www.examsam.com
This material may not be copied or reproduced in any form.

15. The correct answer is A. The most likely rationale behind the issuance of this document is to advise employees to be vigilant when using dangerous substances. The rationale is implied in the first sentence of the document, which states: "The following are ten basic rules that we expect all of our employees who handle or work around hazardous materials always to know and follow." For questions like this, remember to choose a general statement, rather than focusing on specific points in the document.

16. The correct answer is E. If you are not able to find the Safety Data Sheet (SDS) for a chemical that is in a bottle, you should check to see whether information about the substance can be found on the label of the container. Point 6 explains: "Employees handling hazardous materials need to read labels on all chemicals before they use or handle them. This information can be found on the applicable Safety Data Sheet (SDS)." So, the product information can be found on both the product label and on the SDS, but the SDS also deals with "handling and storing materials, as well as with cleaning up spills and providing relevant first-aid when necessary."

17. The correct answer is B. When you are finished using a hazardous substance, you should first check whether any of the substance has leaked out or spilled during use. Obviously, if there were a spill, you would then need to clean it, and to do so safely, you would still need to wear your PPE.

18. The correct answer is A. The most likely rationale behind sections 1 and 2 of the email is to state that advisors must inform clients that L & M has no

© COPYRIGHT 2022. Exam SAM Study Aids & Media dba www.examsam.com
This material may not be copied or reproduced in any form.

liability for investors' losses. The document is addressed to all L & M financial advisors, and begins with the statement that "you must advise clients of the potential risk considerations enumerated in this email before they make any investment with us. So, the document is laying out how staff needs to explain risks to clients, rather than explaining anything to staff. As financial advisors, the representatives would already be aware of the risks of investing.

19. The correct answer is D. If you have purchased a secured corporate bond, but have discovered that the company that you invested in has gone bankrupt, you are likely to get back your money on the investment as long as the company you invested in has made money on the sale of its assets. This scenario is covered in point 8: "When a company goes bankrupt, it pays money back to investors in a particular order as it liquidates. After a company has sold off all its assets, it will pay off its debts, including bonds, first." So if the company gets money from the sale of assets, it will then pay back its bond holders.

20. The correct answer is D. Section 3 states that "the company pays interest and returns the amount invested on the redemption date." Answer B is incorrect because a secured bond can be paid off early, according to section 7. Answer C is incorrect because all bonds are indentures, but only some of them are secured. Answer E is incorrect because the bond could be paid off early by the company, even when the economy is good.

© COPYRIGHT 2022. Exam SAM Study Aids & Media dba www.examsam.com
This material may not be copied or reproduced in any form.

21. The correct answer is D. If an employee takes no days of paid sick leave during the year, they may be eligible to use 3 of those days as personal days next year. Paragraph 4 states: "Employees who experience no illnesses during a particular calendar year are requested to use 3 days of paid sick leave as personal days in the following calendar year." You may be tempted to choose answer B, but the ability to carryforward five sick days to next year would depend on an employee's existing balance from the previous year. Note that both part-time and full-time employees are eligible for sick pay.

22. The correct answer is E. The most likely purpose of the PSPL-5 is to request a specific type of time off. Paragraph 4 of the document explains that "these 3 personal days should be taken from January 1 to January 31 of the following calendar year. The employee must prepare PSPL-5, which must be approved by their department manager." So, the PSPL-5 is the document that an employee prepares to use the 3 personal days, described in the document.

23. The correct answer is B. If a part-time employee who has worked for 15 weeks would like to use some of her sick days for her husband's upcoming operation, you should ask her what dates the operation is to determine if she allowed paid sick leave. The pertinent information from paragraph 2 is as follows: "Paid sick leave accrues to any employee who has worked for the Company for at least [. . .] 60 days as a part-time employee. [. . .] Part-

© COPYRIGHT 2022. Exam SAM Study Aids & Media dba www.examsam.com
This material may not be copied or reproduced in any form.

time employees can begin using accrued sick leave when they have worked for the Company for 90 days." So, at fifteen weeks of work, the part-time employee has worked a maximum of 75 days (15 weeks x 5 days per week = 75). She begins to accrue sick pay after 60 days of work, but can use it only after 90 days of work. So, at the present time, she would not be eligible to use the sick pay. However, if her husband's operation were after the 90-day period (in approximately three weeks or 15 more days of work), she will be eligible to use the sick pay. So, you need to ask for the date of the operation.

24. The correct answer is A. In terms of deciding whether a special packaging standard is reasonable, you do not need to consider the costs in implementing such a standard. The support for this answer can be found in section 3(e): "Nothing in this Act shall be construed to require the Commission, in establishing a standard under this section, to prepare a comparison of the costs that would be incurred in complying with such standard with the benefits of such standard." Note that answer D would be considered as "manufacturing processes" as described in Sec. 3(b)(3) of the document.

25. The correct answer is B. If you have discovered that a major manufacturer of a household substance is selling it in special packaging, marketed as "easy opening" for those with arthritis, you should investigate whether the product has appropriate labeling. The applicable information for section 4(a)

© COPYRIGHT 2022. Exam SAM Study Aids & Media dba www.examsam.com
This material may not be copied or reproduced in any form.

is as follows: "For the purpose of making any household substance [. . .] readily available to elderly or handicapped persons unable to use such substance when packaged in compliance with such standard, the manufacturer [. . .] may package any household substance [. . .] in packaging of a single size which does not comply with such standard if [. . . the package] bears conspicuous labeling stating: 'This package for households without young children.'"

26. The correct answer is A. The most likely purpose of these two sections of the law is to ensure that any danger posed by the packaging of harmful substances is reasonably reduced. The other answer choices state specific points from the document, rather than the general idea. Section 3 states the provisions for the packages, while section 4 provides an exception to these provisions.

27. The correct answer is C. If you have just told a client about a new product, and you do not want the client to share the information with anyone else, you should write to the client to inform them that the information is confidential. Section 1 of the document states: "When Confidential Information is transmitted orally, the Disclosing Party must, after such oral disclosure, promptly provide a written statement to the Receiving Party indicating that said oral communication constitutes Confidential Information."

28. The correct answer is C. If you have discovered that someone who works on a casual basis for the company has posted the details of one of the

© COPYRIGHT 2022. Exam SAM Study Aids & Media dba www.examsam.com
This material may not be copied or reproduced in any form.

company's new designs online, you should determine whether the information was received in a legitimate manner. Section 2(b), which explains the exclusions to the policy, points out that "the obligations of the Receiving Party (the worker) [. . .] shall exclude information that is [. . .] (b) discovered by the Receiving Party through legitimate means."

29. The correct answer is D. As mentioned in section 4 of the document, the USTPO is most likely to be an organization that deals with trade secrets. Section 4 states that confidentiality "shall remain in effect until the Confidential Information no longer qualifies as a trade secret as defined by the USPTO." If the USTPO is establishing how a trade secret is defined, then it must be an organization that regularly deals with trade secrets.

30. The correct answer is A. The explanation that best describes the phrase "remain open for execution" from paragraph 1 is that the LOI will be legally-binding if the contract is signed before June 21, 2023. Paragraph 1 states: "This LOI will remain open for execution by the other party for six months after the date indicated in Paragraph D." Paragraph D indicates the date December 21, 2022. So, June 21, 2023 is 6 months after December 21, 2022. Note that "executing" a contract means that it is signed by all parties, thereby becoming legally valid and binding.

31. The correct answer is D. An acceptable reason for terminating the LOI would be that the buyer has breached the terms of the LOI. Section D of the document states: "the termination of the Binding Provisions due to a breach

© COPYRIGHT 2022. Exam SAM Study Aids & Media dba www.examsam.com
This material may not be copied or reproduced in any form.

of the terms of the LOI by either party shall not affect the liability of a party for breach of any of said Binding Provisions."

32. The correct answer is E. If you have found out that the Buyer is looking at purchasing a grocery store from another party, in addition to the motel they are purchasing from you, you should take no action. Section B talks about exclusive dealings between the seller and the buyer. Specifically, Section B(ii) explains that the "buyer will not enter into any negotiations or agreements for the purpose of buying or exchanging any real property, other than the Premises, to be used by Buyer for the purpose for which Buyer seeks to purchase the Premises." The key phrase in this clause is "to be used by Buyer for the purpose for which Buyer seeks to purchase the Premises." The buyer is purchasing a motel from the seller. Since a grocery store has a completely different purpose than a motel, the exclusive dealings clause has not been broken and no action needs to be taken.

33. The correct answer is B. If a customer wishes to object to part of a contract for $1,000 worth of goods to you that they signed 5 weeks ago, you should refute the objection since too much time has elapsed. Subsection 2 explains that "notice of objection to its (the sales contract's) contents" must be "given within ten days after it is received." The contact was signed 5 weeks ago, so too much time has passed for the customer to make an objection.

34. The correct answer is C. If you are nearly finished manufacturing a special order for a customer of goods that cannot otherwise be sold on the open

© COPYRIGHT 2022. Exam SAM Study Aids & Media dba www.examsam.com
This material may not be copied or reproduced in any form.

market, and the customer tells you they want to cancel the order, you should inform the customer that the order may not be canceled. Subsection (3)(a) clarifies that a contract is valid "if the goods are to be specially manufactured for the buyer and are not suitable for sale to others in the ordinary course of the seller's business and the seller [. . .] has made [. . .] a substantial beginning of their manufacture or commitments for their procurement."

35. The correct answer is A. If you have entered into a sales contract with a buyer of goods priced at $550, and you have noticed that the customer's last name is misspelled, the contract will not be considered insufficient. Subsection (1) states: "A writing is not insufficient because it omits or incorrectly states a term agreed upon."

© COPYRIGHT 2022. Exam SAM Study Aids & Media dba www.examsam.com
This material may not be copied or reproduced in any form.

Answers and Explanations – Practice Test 3

1. The correct answer is C. The main purpose of the document is to explain the circumstances in which certain goods can be returned. We know this because the title of the document is "Store Return Policy" and only certain items are mentioned in the policy. Answer B is too broad, and answers A, D, and E are specific points from the document, rather than the main purpose.

2. The correct answer is A. The first paragraph states that swimwear "as before, cannot be returned in any circumstance as per state health and hygiene laws." Swimwear is an exception to the normal policies on sporting goods returns, so answers B and C are incorrect for this reason.

3. The correct answer is A. The insurance would cover the company if it loses income because part of the factory is damaged. The second point of the document states that "business losses due to temporarily stopping operations because of property being damaged are covered." The situations mentioned in the other answer choices are not covered because answer B is an intentional act, and answers C, D, and E are foreseeable events.

4. The correct answer is E. "By pretermission" in the last paragraph is closest in meaning to "by negligence." Remember to look for synonyms in the same paragraph for these types of questions. The first sentence of the "Exclusions" paragraph states: "Any expense or loss which is not accidental or which is foreseen is excluded from our policy." The second sentence of

© COPYRIGHT 2022. Exam SAM Study Aids & Media dba www.examsam.com
This material may not be copied or reproduced in any form.

that paragraph states: "In other words, damage caused intentionally or by pretermission is not covered." So, "not accidental" is synonymous with "intentional" and "which is foreseen" relates to the word "pretermission." So, if a company can foresee than a problem is going to occur and they do nothing about it, they would probably be considered guilty of negligence by the insurance company.

5. The correct answer is B. If the coin incorrectly falls into the "reject" channel, the technician should first check the deflector. Point 4 says that "if the deflector is functional, the coin should fall into the 'accept' instead of the 'reject' channel." So, if the coin is incorrectly rejected, the problem could lie with the deflector.

6. The correct answer is B. The instructions explain that "if coins decrease in speed on the runway, the coin is considered real, meaning that the magnets are functioning correctly." So, both the magnets and the runway are used in determining the authenticity of the coin.

7. The correct answer is D. In paragraph 4, the word "nominal" most nearly means being so-named. The phrase "pay growth gate" is included in quotation marks in paragraph 4, indicating that the phrase has been coined. Note that nominal can also mean a small amount when used in other contexts.

8. The correct answer is A. According to the document, if the number of highly-paid jobs suddenly goes up, this may have a disproportionate effect on the

© COPYRIGHT 2022. Exam SAM Study Aids & Media dba www.examsam.com
This material may not be copied or reproduced in any form.

pay growth rate percentage. The final paragraph explains that "The earnings estimates are not just a measure of pay rises as they also reflect [. . .] changes in the structure of the workforce. For example, more highly-paid jobs would have an upward effect on earnings growth rates." If more highly-paid jobs are included in the figure, the pay growth rate, which would be calculated as the total increase in pay divided by the number of employees, would be skewed because the pay growth would be divided by a lower figure.

9. The correct answer is E. According to the document, average billing is intended to help customers better plan for payment of their electricity bills. The first paragraph of the document states: "By using average billing, a customer should be able to have a predictable electric bill, similar to their other monthly expenditures like rent or insurance."

10. The correct answer is C. The acronym MkWh in the last paragraph of the document most likely refers to the rate of the customer's monthly electricity usage. We have seen the acronym kWh previously in the document, which is used to refer to the rate of a customer's usage of electricity in general. The final paragraph points out: "In the event that a customer wishes to revise their monthly bills, their MkWh must have been steadily declining for at least 6 months." Since this paragraph uses both the words "monthly" and "month," we can conclude that MkWh is the monthly rate of usage.

© COPYRIGHT 2022. Exam SAM Study Aids & Media dba www.examsam.com
This material may not be copied or reproduced in any form.

11. The correct answer is B. If you work as an auditor for the State Department of Revenue, your primary rationale behind sending this document would be to receive payment for any payroll taxes that may be outstanding. As an auditor, your primary job would be to collect any potential outstanding income owing to the state. The activities mentioned in the other answer choices would be secondary to this.

12. The correct answer is C. If the company has not already sent in a return, they may not be required to file one or they may now need to do so. If they need to file one, they need to "prepare the enclosed return and send it back to us using the pre-addressed envelope provided," as stated under the first heading of the letter. If the company does not need to file a return, they need to send in an "explanation and copies of the requested returns," as stated under the last heading of the letter. So in either case, the company has to send in an explanation and/or the requested returns.

13. The correct answer is A. The acronym UIM in Document A most likely refers to a written manual with instructions on how to use the sealant machine. Document A states that after adjusting the sealant time, "the sealant machine should now be operational and fully functional to use on any materials that conform those stated in the UIM." The words "stated in" and "conforms to" imply that these are instructions in a manual or booklet.

14. The correct answer is B. According to both documents, turning the control knob clockwise while holding button B is the last required step in adjusting

© COPYRIGHT 2022. Exam SAM Study Aids & Media dba www.examsam.com
This material may not be copied or reproduced in any form.

sealant time. Document B, which addresses the adjustment of sealant time, explains that "in the event that sealant time needs to be adjusted, then turn the control knob that reads "Sealant Time" to the right (clockwise) while simultaneously depressing button B."

15. The correct answer is C. According to the document, an item is considered to be accepted if the customer makes modifications to it. Point 2 of the "Repair and replacements" section of the document states that "a customer has accepted an item [if they have . . .] altered the item."

16. The correct answer is D. If there is a request for repairs or replacements less than six months after the purchase of an item, the Company must repair or replace the item, unless it has evidence that it was working when the customer bought it. Paragraph 3 of the "Repair and replacements" section of the document states that "the company must repair or replace an item if a customer returns it within 6 months, unless the Company can prove it was not faulty when the customer purchased it."

17. The correct answer is E. You should advise the customer that they need to send permission for the return via text or email to their friend. The final paragraph explains that "friends, family members, or other third parties wishing to return an item on behalf of the customer must first present permission from the customer in the form of a written statement." A text or email satisfies the requirement that the communication be written; a telephone call does not.

© COPYRIGHT 2022. Exam SAM Study Aids & Media dba www.examsam.com
This material may not be copied or reproduced in any form.

18. The correct answer is D. The phrase "automatic approval rights" in paragraph 3 of the document implies that managers don't need to sign online claims under $100. Paragraph 3 states: "Some managers have automatic approval rights for online claim submissions which are less than $100 only, circumventing the need for a signature and signatory rights form." "Circumvent" means to avoid having to do something.

19. The correct answer is E. The employee will not be granted more time to make corrections to an incomplete or illegible expense claim form. Paragraph 2 states that "the normal cut-off time will apply to the corrected expense claim form."

20. The correct answer is C. According to the document, if you receive an expense claim form for a $90 expenditure that was made by the employee four months ago, you should deny the claim because it has been filed too late. The last paragraph explains that "expense claims for expenditures more than three months old will not be paid under any circumstances."

21. The correct answer is A. According to the document, a person who works for the company on a casual, as-needed basis can be excluded from the 401(k) plan. Paragraph 1 of the document explains that the rules of the plan apply to all employees, regardless of whether they are "classified as being employed on a full-time, part-time, short-term, or long-term basis." However, a casual, as-needed worker would not be considered an employee, but rather an independent contractor.

© COPYRIGHT 2022. Exam SAM Study Aids & Media dba www.examsam.com
This material may not be copied or reproduced in any form.

22. The correct answer is B. Factors that apply exclusively to the Company, like its historical financial performance, may affect the Company's contribution rate to the plan. Section 1.1 states: "State and Federal regulation of 401(k) plans [. . .] may take into account factors such as the unique needs of the employer establishing the plan." The financial performance of a company would qualify as a unique need under section 1.1 of the document.

23. The correct answer is A. The phrase "portability rights" in section 1.2 of the document means that an employee can move the money from the plan to new employer's plan. This is also mentioned in section 1.4, which describes protections against "suspension of portability upon termination." Answer choices B, C, and D are incorrect because there would be no need to move the plan if the employee is still employed by the company. The information in answer E is not stated in the document.

24. The correct answer is B. Before the date of the merger, ABC needs to deliver any documents to the surviving corporation if they request them. This is stated in the last sentence of the document.

25. The correct answer is A. If another company has a lawsuit against ABC on the date of the merger, ABC will remain liable for any action under the lawsuit. The last paragraph states: "Any action or proceeding either pending by or against ABC (such as a lawsuit) may be prosecuted to judgment as if the merger had not taken place," in other words, as though ABC still exited.

© COPYRIGHT 2022. Exam SAM Study Aids & Media dba www.examsam.com
This material may not be copied or reproduced in any form.

26. The correct answer is C. The last sentence of the second paragraph states: "all rights of creditors and all liens upon the property of ABC shall be preserved unimpaired, and all debts, liabilities, obligations, and duties of ABC shall attach to the surviving corporation, and may be enforced against it to the same extent as if the debts, liabilities, obligations, and duties had been incurred or contracted by it." A loan on the property constitutes a right of a creditor. The clause states that the obligation "shall attach to the surviving corporation," meaning that it becomes the responsibility of the surviving corporation.

27. The correct answer is E. According to the document, when a resident's absence from the Country is under two years, they will not have to reapply for permission to remain in the Country. The section of the document entitled "Less than 2 years' absence" states: "A person who has been absent from the Country for less than 2 years will retain their permission to remain in the Country and will not need to apply for entry [. . .] before returning to their residence."

28. The correct answer is D. According to the document, the phrase "grandfather clause" in paragraph 3 refers to the exception provided for residence obtained before January 1, 1975. The section of the document entitled "2 years' or more absence" points out that "the exception to this (losing permission to remain) is only for residents who took up residence in the Country prior to January 1, 1975. Such residents are protected from

118

© COPYRIGHT 2022. Exam SAM Study Aids & Media dba www.examsam.com
This material may not be copied or reproduced in any form.

losing permission to remain in the Country due to absences outside the Country until December 31, 2035, when this grandfather clause shall be revoked." Since the sentence containing the phrase "grandfather clause" comes immediately after the sentence which describes the exception, we can infer that the phrase is referring to the exception.

29. The correct answer is A. The most likely rationale of the last paragraph of the document is to allow more generous residency rules for families providing service to the Country in some way. The paragraph refers to family members of a member of the Armed Forces overseas; [. . .] a High-Level Diplomat [. . .]; or those who have been employed overseas as foreign employees of the country."

30. The correct answer is C. The most likely explanation of the phrase "Apis mellifera adansonii" in Section 284(b) of the document is that it is a particular species or subspecies of honeybees. This section covers the "prevention or retardation of the spread of undesirable pathogens, including but not limited to those from Apis mellifera adansonii." We know that this is a type of honeybee because a pathogen or disease would not originate from the things mentioned in the other answer choices. In addition, the genus "Apis" has already been explained in Section 281(d).

31. The correct answer is B. According to the document, the Secretary of the Treasury is involved in governing the importation of honeybees by establishing rules and regulations for these types of importations. Section

© COPYRIGHT 2022. Exam SAM Study Aids & Media dba www.examsam.com
This material may not be copied or reproduced in any form.

281(c) discusses the "regulations promulgated by [. . .] the Secretary of the Treasury."

32. The correct answer is D. A shipment of Columbian honeybees about to arrive in the United States needs to be checked to see whether the importation conforms to the promulgated regulations. Although we can see in the last paragraph of the document that the US cooperates with Columbia to carry out research, any honeybee imports from Columbia would still need to be checked under the rules stated in section 281 of the document.

33. The correct answer is A. The phrase "Introduced Client' as it is used in the document refers to a party who hires someone after meeting that person via the Introducer. According to section 1.2: "If following the making of an Introduction, an Introduced Client engages the Client within 12 months of the introduction, for the provision of its services" a fee becomes payable by the Introduced Client for the introduction. So, an Introduced Client meets the client through the Introducer. Note that answers B and C are incorrect because the clients could be introduced without becoming engaged in a work relationship, and a commission would not be payable in that instance.

34. The correct answer is C. According to the document, a year plus one month and 21 days would be the maximum number of days from the date of introduction that an Introducer would need to wait for Payment, without late fees being incurred. According to section 1.2, an Introduced Client is able to engage a Client up to 12 months after the introduction. Section 1.4 states

© COPYRIGHT 2022. Exam SAM Study Aids & Media dba www.examsam.com
This material may not be copied or reproduced in any form.

that the fee for the introduction will be invoiced at the end of the month, and section 1.5 explains that invoices need to be raised within 7 days. Section 1.6 adds that "payment shall be made . . . within 14 days." So, adding these all together, we get a year plus one month and 21 days.

35. The correct answer is A. If you discover that an Introduced Client engaged one of your clients fourteen months ago without informing you, and the Introduced Client claims that they do not intend pay you any introductory commission, you should first determine the amount of fees paid by the Introduced Party to the Engaged Party during its first 12 months of service. You would need to do this to quantify damages in order to undertake legal action against the Introduced Client for breaking the contract.

© COPYRIGHT 2022. Exam SAM Study Aids & Media dba www.examsam.com
This material may not be copied or reproduced in any form.

© COPYRIGHT 2022. Exam SAM Study Aids & Media dba www.examsam.com
This material may not be copied or reproduced in any form.

www.ingramcontent.com/pod-product-compliance
Lightning Source LLC
Chambersburg PA
CBHW080421030426
42335CB00020B/2537